DEBRIEF TO WIN

HOW AMERICA'S TOP GUNS PRACTICE ACCOUNTABLE LEADERSHIP... AND HOW YOU CAN, TOO!

ROBERT "CUJO" TESCHNER

RTI Press

A VMax Group Imprint

www.vmaxgroupllc.com

Cover images: © Shutterstock.com
Cover design: Alexander Vulchev
Interior layout design: Jennifer Woodhead

Published by RTI Press
A VMax Group, LLC imprint, Chesterfield, Missouri, USA.

Library of Congress Cataloging-in-Publication Data:
Names: Teschner, Robert, author.
Title: Debrief to Win: How America's Top Guns Practice Accountable Leadership...and How You Can, Too! / Robert "Cujo" Teschner
Description: First edition. | Chesterfield: RTI Press, 2018.
Identifiers: ISBN: 978-1-7329298-0-7 (Hardcover) | ISBN: 978-1-7329298-1-4 (Softcover) | ISBN 978-1-7329298-2-1 (E book) | ISBN: 978-1-7329298-3-8 (Audio book)
Subjects: LCSH: Accountability. | Accountable leadership. | Teamwork. | Teams. | Organizational effectiveness. | Leadership.

Printed in the United States of America

10 9 8 7 6 5 4 3 2 1

I dedicate this book first of all to my dearest Diane,
My beautiful and caring bride—
who saved my life from cancer by insisting on a second opinion.

I could not have found a better partner and friend.
You love me without question;
Most importantly—you love and care for our five beautiful children,
who are my other true joys in this life!

I furthermore dedicate this book to my precious children;
I pray that someday our journey from 2014 to now makes abundant sense.
To Michael, Christopher, Lucy, Stephen and Nicholas,
All My Love, Dad

"There is no limit to the good you can do
if you don't care who gets the credit."

General George C. Marshall, USA

"In matters of principle, stand like a rock; in matters of taste,
swim with the current. Give up money, give up fame, give
up science, give up earth itself and all it contains, rather
than do an immoral act. And never suppose that in any
situation, or under any circumstances, it is best for you
to do a dishonorable thing.

Whenever you are to do a thing, though it can never be known but
to yourself, ask yourself how you would act were all the world
looking at you, and act accordingly."

President Thomas Jefferson

CONTENTS

PART TWO
THE ART OF THE DEBRIEF

FOREWORD

When I first entered the Army back in the late 1950's, I had no idea what my first experience would be. As I walked into Boot Camp, oblivious to my insignificance, I met for the very first time a man who I was to only know then and to remember to this day as 'Sergeant.'

I don't remember his name.

I only remember his presence–and that I had never met anyone who took himself and his job so seriously. So determined. So tall. So straight up and down. So *serious*.

That's what struck me when I first met Colonel Rob Teschner, the author of this most remarkable book. What struck me was his seriousness.

Not the kind of seriousness we all think of when we use that word, but the kind of serious that my Sergeant wore every single moment of the time I spent with him and he spent with me.

In the case of Rob Teschner, known as "Cujo" to his people, it's "Top Gun" serious.

It's the kind of serious that's born out of a deeply learned truth that every action we take in life is a life and death action.

That people depend upon us.

That outcomes aren't just those which come about because of some haphazard decision we made, but that outcomes bear consequences more significant than anything we can imagine.

Cujo—who spent his life as a Top Gun fighter pilot, an

operational F-22 "Raptor" squadron commander, and finally a senior member of a Combatant Command staff—considered nothing more serious than the decisions he and his people made every single moment of every single day, when performing their missions.

But it wasn't just what happened up in the air. It's what happened every single time when Cujo and his team returned to base.

Cujo learned and mastered, because he had to, *The Art of the Debrief.*

He knew that every single sortie would become an exercise, not only in fulfilling the mission, but in learning how to do it better the very next time.

And that's what this book is about.

Its goal is to bring you the extreme seriousness that distinguishes the heroes in our lives.

The intense focus called for to excel beyond the ordinary.

The intense love for the role we have been gifted to play in the fulfillment of our various life missions.

As you read this book, know that you're in the presence of a hero.

That's all I need to say to you about what's coming next.

Listen. Learn. Debrief.

Michael E. Gerber
Author of the E-Myth series

MISSION ESSENTIALS

WHAT IS A DEBRIEF?

"A debrief is the process of constructively evaluating the quality of the decisions everyone on the team made from planning through execution, in relation to the objectives the team set out to achieve."

BY THE WAY:

*A debrief is **not** a gruesome sport or a place of blame or shame. Quite the opposite, in fact the debrief is **where we celebrate our victories** as well as **learn from our failures**. We do this in order to build cohesive teams and improve moving forward. A debrief properly run is an affirming, positive experience. It is also where we begin the practice of Accountable Leadership.*

PREFACE

"

FAILURE IS SIMPLY THE OPPORTUNITY TO
BEGIN AGAIN, THIS TIME MORE
INTELLIGENTLY.

Henry Ford

For those of you who might wonder why I wrote this book, three drivers compelled me to do so. To begin with, I love teaching. I taught professionally throughout my Air Force career, and I find it immensely satisfying. When I retired from the Air Force, it became clear to me that my mission was to guide others how to maximize their success in business and in life. I use the core fighter pilot approach to achieving mission success to teach this.

My career as a fighter pilot is my inspiration for this approach. First, I hope to leave a legacy of transforming the state of business for the better, allowing companies and organizations everywhere to collectively raise their game. Beyond the joy I experience in teaching this way, the mission behind it is absolutely critical. Businesses small and large *must* succeed. The economic backbone of our country fuels everything else; without a vibrant economy all of us have less security and more threats that cause our overall quality of life to deteriorate quickly. To that end, not only must individual enterprise succeed; but, given the increasingly inter-connected economic world in which we live, businesses *everywhere* must succeed. We've recently survived the Great Recession, and recognize the massive challenges this posed. It is my goal to play a small part in ensuring we can prevent a future recession from taking such a toll.

Second, while high-performing military teams routinely use "debriefs" to improve team performance quickly, civilian businesses tend to gloss over mistakes. Companies in general have a habit of saying, "Well, we won't go there again," without really analyzing *why* that strategy or business plan failed. Furthermore, while some material has been written about the utility of debriefs, it's rarely written by those who *practiced* this art professionally. Those in the military who practice debriefing do so with *literally everything on the line*!

For reference, project management practitioners write a lot about "Project Retrospectives". This is a form of debrief used in various communities around the world. While this form of debrief fills a need and serves as a solid starting point, it leaves much to be desired. The few books in circulation that touch on high-performing team versions of the debrief offer some nuggets of great information. But these books often don't tackle the subject of the debrief to the level necessary to either overcome the natural "institutional antibodies"—the "not invented here" kinds of criticism that pop up in response. Current debrief writing does nothing to help someone with little to no experience in this field learn to practice this art successfully on their own.

Debrief to Win aims to fix this by filling this void.

The approach centered on debriefing ultimately aims at helping organizations practice something called Accountable Leadership, one that is based on a tried, tested and winning methodology. Without Accountable Leadership, businesses lose billions of dollars in unattained revenue, and waste countless resources.

The world is changing at an incredible and almost alarming rate. The amount of information to which people have access is growing exponentially. For ordinary people, this level of access is overwhelming the traditional processes by which business leaders transmit and receive information, both from the marketplace and from their own employees. When toy giant Toys "R" Us declared bankruptcy in the Spring of 2018, it joined the ranks of the bastions of American business that lost by not being agile enough to keep up with the times. In short, they sold physical toys from physical buildings in an age when play is becoming increasingly electronic, and parents are purchasing toys from online outlets.

Sears, once the largest retailer in the United States, is in the process of closing dozens of stores. By mid-2018, it had already closed half of its physical locations in the past five years.[1] Sears should have "debriefed" and learned from its own success: the company arose through an earlier version of the internet—the U.S. Mail, delivering products via catalog to rural areas that could not be served by physical stores. Now, Sears itself is under attack from a new delivery model. How and why is a company, as renowned and once-beloved as Sears closing locations across America and quickly losing lots of money? And why have 67 executives at the vice-president level or higher, left within the past couple of years?

Most importantly, did Sears engage in critical self-examination? According to a recent Business Insider online article, "There are so many people running for the door, not just because the ship is sinking, but because the captain of the ship is screaming at them, blaming it on them, and telling them it's their fault."[2] It's a sad state of affairs…and, unfortunately, one that is not exclusive to Sears.

When I scan the environment for resources that leaders can use to learn to make better decisions I'm frustrated by what I find. So much current leadership training is created and/or taught by those who haven't actually lived it. A great deal of what's available is informed by pseudo-science and personal theories that may sound good or look promising on paper, but don't stand up to a more rigorous test. My approach has always been this: pick the person or team who knows how to win, study them well, then replicate what they do, if their success is based on sound practice. Our military knows how to win. Constantly. Overwhelmingly. If you study our incredible military, you will learn how to win too.

My introduction to leadership training started in 2004, when I was assigned the position of "Core Debrief Instructor" for the USAF Weapons School—the renowned Air Force "Top Gun" school. I was given the "Keys of the Kingdom," with the mandate to teach the entire school—*all* of the various disciplines, from Space, to Intelligence, to Helicopters, to Transports, to Fighters, and all disciplines in between—how to master *The Art of the Debrief.*

It was a challenging task, because my team had to overcome institutional resistance; that is, each community had its own way of doing things. We had to agree on a standardized vocabulary, since each community had its own way of talking about doing things. And we had to be able to generate consistent results; meaning, each community had to learn how to integrate with the others. At the same time, my friends working in industry were constantly sharing stories about the absence of accountability in their organizations.

My mind was set—I knew that what I would come to call *The Debrief-Focused Approach™* was going to be *THE* tool, the vital framework that businesses could use to learn how to improve, and I've been passionate about this approach ever since.

More importantly, I came to realize that *The Debrief-Focused Approach™* is, in a nutshell, **the essence of Accountable Leadership.** It's more than just the smart way to do things. It's the full scope of the accountable leadership system we practice in high-performing military teams that allows us to dominate in combat and train our leaders to do their absolute best. Although I didn't realize it at the time, I learned how to teach Accountable Leadership as a brand-new Instructor Pilot at the Air Force Weapons School. I am forever grateful for that incredible opportunity, and to the great leaders in my life who helped get me there.

Taking on the Establishment

A while back, an outstanding client of mine introduced me to a very experienced, well-established leadership consultant. After we finished the initial pleasantries, the consultant asked me a series of questions about the work I'm doing and the approach we're using. He ended his questioning with a final and interesting query, "If this approach is so good, why haven't I heard of it?"

Let me begin by affirming that I am not at all surprised by this. I recognize that inherent in every business is a form of conflict; a battle for resources, clients, attention, validation. Most critically, current approaches to leadership training aren't always worth the extremely high prices companies are paying, and the time that they and their people are investing.

Additionally, the leadership training world is rife with fads, "sure-fire" approaches to success, and people promising to transform an organization, from the bottom-up, in no time at all. The question then becomes: how good is leadership today? How effective are current approaches? What return on investment are organizations getting?

According to Jeffrey Pfeffer, a professor at Stanford University's Graduate School of Business, "…despite the billions of dollars that companies spend on developing their leaders through training programs, inspirational keynote speeches, conferences, and coaching engagements, leadership isn't any stronger today."[3] Furthermore, Pfeffer notes, "…part of the problem is that anyone can be a self-proclaimed leadership expert in today's world. One doesn't even need any relevant experience."[4] Pfeffer's research suggests that some of the top leadership "experts" have "little to no" experience as actual leaders. Yet they are accepted as authorities because "they had all written leadership books and all did a lot of public speaking."[5]

Therefore, to answer the leadership consultant's questions about why he'd never heard of this method, I pointed out that all of the components of *The Debrief-Focused Approach*™ are already in the marketplace. There are other former leaders of high-performing teams out there teaching the methodologies that truly work, to companies and organizations that genuinely want to improve their leaders' capabilities. The reality is that there's huge demand for high-performing team training and the associated skill sets; the problem is that there are so few qualified practitioners available to teach it.

The simple fact is that what my team and I teach is more than an expensive two-day certification course in leadership — which is the usual route taken by leadership coaches, "Agile" practitioners and others in this space. The methodologies I share with you in this book are those I lived by, and worked very hard to **become qualified to teach**, during my career as a fighter pilot, Air Force Weapons School Instructor, and commander of one of our nation's front-line operational F-22 "Raptor" squadrons.

These skills have become part of my DNA and inform the way that I look at the world. My hope is that this book helps you and your organization develop in the same way, to your tremendous benefit.

How *Debrief to Win* Will Dramatically Improve Your Company

To begin with, I want to share with you how to organize and equip your teams to be able to debrief. That's the whole point of the first section of this book, one which must be in place in order for the debrief tool to be effective. Then I intend to arm you with this incredibly effective tool that you can use to your *significant advantage* in both business and life. Like any tool, it can be used to great effect; or it can be misused and even abused, which is a point many fail to recognize.

Please note that *not all debriefs are good*, even some that sound and feel right. It's easy leave a poorly-executed debrief feeling great, despite the fact that you've walked away <u>armed with the wrong answers to equally wrong questions</u>. This can be extremely costly to your organization across the board. I aim to teach you how to use this tool to your constant advantage, and I want you to see how effective it can be in strengthening your business position. Debriefing *correctly and consistently* will positively affect your bottom-line to dramatic effect (spoiler alert: we're talking about a potential 20+% increase in effectiveness) for those who practice this approach properly.[6]

In addition to helping you apply this skill set to your organization, I want you to stretch beyond the obvious and start developing a life-skill that helps you to really improve your health and well-being, your relationships, your spirituality—any important area of your life. The full approach I'm suggesting here is what I call *The Debrief Focused Approach*™, but for now know that the Debrief methodology I'm sharing with you in *Debrief to Win* has the power to *fundamentally transform lives*. I know, because I've learned this lesson the hard way.

Finally, while many of the concepts I'm sharing here have their obvious parallels in the business world (I'll highlight many of these as we go), we'll always fall back on the fighter pilot approach to debriefing throughout this book. This isn't aimed to distract, but rather to show you where the process comes from and how it's applied by our airborne warriors.

I don't intend to soften any language to make this more "business-y." This book is written by a fighter pilot about the warrior approach we use to win in combat. It's what I believe you thought you'd get when you heard about this book, and it's the approach I think you'll appreciate when you're through.

Robert "Cujo" Teschner
St. Louis, Missouri
October 2018

DEBRIEF
TO WIN

"
___

IN BUSINESS, TRIBES ARE OFTEN SOCIAL
GROUPS LINKED BY A LEADER, SHARED
PURPOSE OR GOAL, COMMON CULTURE
OR ORGANIZATIONAL BOUNDARY.

Soren Eilertsen
The Nature of Business Tribes[7]

INTRODUCTION

THE URGENT NEED FOR ACCOUNTABLE LEADERSHIP

IF YOU WANT TO BE HUGELY SUCCESSFUL...
YOU HAVE TO STAY HUGELY HUMBLE.

"It's Not About You,"
Burg and Mann

It was an important day for me in my evolution as a fighter pilot. It was an "upgrade ride" day—a critical mission as part of my qualification program to become the lead fighter pilot of a team of four. We call this a 4-Ship Flight Lead, and it's an important role for a fighter pilot. It is where you receive the authority to lead three other pilots, with their fully-armed aircraft, into combat. It means demonstrating the ability to not only plan appropriately, but also to brief (i.e., explain) the plan to the other members of the team and then safely lead the mission. Most importantly, this responsibility involves keeping track of everyone else and how they're doing—all the while doing your own job with a high degree of precision. It's akin to the job of a quarterback in the National Football League; you must know not only your own assignment, but all the routes of all the receivers and all of the blocking assignments—except with far more serious consequences.

Don't Repeat Your Mistakes

Imagine the chaos of air combat—everyone on both sides of the conflict flying at speeds faster than sound, missiles flying on both sides, from the ground and in the air, urgent radio calls from everyone within the formation, with each pilot frantically trying to explain who's "locked" to who, who's shooting who, who's defensive and defending themselves—with overlapping communications from airborne controllers who are there to help us understand the fight. In the midst of the utter chaos, it's the Flight Lead who's responsible for keeping track of everything; whether or not the team is handling their responsibilities appropriately, ensuring everyone has enough fuel to get home safely, handling systems problems in-flight, tracking where your formation is in relation to the strike package (aircraft) you're protecting—and the myriad other factors that come into play in aerial battle. The most important part of the mission? Getting everyone back safely.

On that particular day, our mission was to escort a fictional "strike package" to the target area and back. Our "strike package" was simulated by one of our team members flying the famous F-15 "Eagle." His job was simply to fly his route and make certain radio calls along the way, reporting his progress to and through the target area. My job, on the other hand, was to ensure that he got there and back safely, while also ensuring *my* team was always in the best position to support him. Fortunately, my "Assistant Flight Lead" was a former Fighter Weapons School Instructor. I was confident of our success.

The mission started off fine. The weather was good, we were where we needed to be at the start, and our airplanes were all performing as designed. We entered "bad guy" airspace at the right time. Shortly thereafter, however, things began to go wrong.

On that particular day we were flying in a large over-water training area that we shared with another US Air Force base. Our airspace was part of a range that had numerous divisions; our portion of the airspace was the furthest South of three chunks, and there were simultaneous training flights happening in all three. As we pushed forward to clear a path for our strike package, my understanding of the battle space started deteriorating rapidly—and so did my Assistant Flight Lead's (also referred to as my "#3"). My wingman and I were focused on our targeting responsibilities, but our targets maneuvered and caused us problems. In trying to figure out how to deal with our responsibilities I quickly lost track of aircraft numbers 3 and 4, as well as their targeting responsibilities. I realized that I was rapidly becoming overwhelmed—"task saturated" is what we call it in fighter terms—and I wasn't yet equipped to deal with such a complex problem.

Mistake #1

I resorted to what I did know—how to lead two aircraft. I focused on myself and my wingman, and I abdicated my responsibilities to my numbers 3 and 4. I found myself hoping that they would do what they needed to do on their own. In short, *I effectively stopped leading them.* Before long, we all became aware that 3 and 4 were flying in the wrong airspace and were targeting members of another fight, one that had absolutely nothing to do with ours. On my side, a couple of enemy aircraft maneuvered past us and were targeting the strike package—the only thing we were supposed to protect, the reason for our mission!

I was stunned. I knew that I had blown it, and in a big way. No fewer than nine members of my squadron (four on my side and five on our "enemies'" side) all received real-time feedback that I was leading an already-failed mission. One of those nine was my Operations Officer, someone whose respect and validation I desperately sought.

Mistake #2

In the debrief, an event designed specifically to help us all improve, I found myself dwelling on all of the errors I made. The debrief I led on the ground quickly devolved into the same type of catastrophe that I had led in the air. Even though I took full responsibility for our team's failure, *this approach only emphasized our mistakes, of which I found plenty.* To make matters worse, I actually shared with my teammates that this was perhaps the worst mission I had ever been on. I openly acknowledged that I led us miserably, and shared that I was incredibly disappointed in myself. But I also shared how disappointed I was in our team for not doing better on a day when we should have easily and completely dominated. I left us all feeling horrible about our under-performance. In short, I crushed my team.

Don't Let Mistake #2 Lead to a Repeat of Mistake #1

I was exceedingly fortunate in that my instructor that day offered a profound analysis of our mission, one that influenced the way I approached debriefs from then on. In just a few minutes, he outlined how a short radio call at this or that critical point could have made a major impact on our success. He shared how, with just a touch more leadership on my part, our team could have rallied with plenty of time to do what was necessary, protecting the strike package as planned. His perspective showed *just how close to success we really were*, and he advised me of how confident he was in my ability to lead when I re-flew that ride the next time. He turned the debrief into a positive, uplifting experience, where I learned how to do better, *where I learned how to win*. Most importantly, he put the focus squarely on the *Root Causes* of our errors, as opposed to the emotional pain I was verbalizing. In effect, he salvaged the debrief by teaching me how to coach my own teams in the future. He helped build me into a firm advocate for our "tribe," and a skilled member of our squadron team. He dramatically improved my skill set and did so in less than 30 minutes.

> " WE SAW OUR DEBRIEFS FOR WHAT THEY TRULY ARE: THE SINGLE MOST IMPORTANT PART OF EACH AND EVERY MISSION, THE PLACE WHERE WE LEARN HOW TO DO BETTER THE NEXT TIME AROUND IN THE CONSTANT EFFORT TO IMPROVE OUR SKILLS AND PREPARE TO WIN IN COMBAT

It took me a long time to learn how to do this half as well as he did, but the lesson was never lost on me, and it resonates to this day. I'll always be thankful to Lt Col Ken "Mach" Tatum for this invaluable lesson.

The Culture and Structure of Our Organization Set Us Up to Win

What's equally important to note from the example above is that our squadron was designed with improvement in mind. We enjoyed a work environment where every member of the team felt "Psychological Safety"—the freedom to express the truth without fear or negative consequences. We valued knowing the truth of what happened while airborne, so that we could identify the Root Causes of our successes and failures. We employed Standards, Tactics and Checklists that served as the foundation for our efforts, documentation that we could be refer to in our post-mission debriefs as the sources of what *should* have been happening. Most importantly, we didn't blame or shame each other in our debriefs—quite the opposite. We saw our debriefs for what they truly are: the single most important part of each and every mission, the place where we learn how to do better the next time around in the constant effort to improve our skills and prepare to win in combat. Our debriefs were tough, and they stung; but they helped us sharpen the iron and develop into the force we are today. And we absolutely took all of this for granted; it's just the way we did our work. It was an intrinsic part of our "tribe's" DNA.

The Desperate Need for Accountable Leadership Training

In the third edition of his book *The Leadership Contract*, author Vince Molinaro highlights a study his company conducted in 2015 on the status of leadership accountability in North

America. His team spoke to HR leaders and senior executives across a variety of industries, asking their impressions of leadership accountability in their companies. The results of this first such study were shocking: "…only 37 percent of respondents were satisfied with the level of leadership accountability in their organizations."[8] Armed with these results, Molinaro then looked at the same issue worldwide. Globally, only 31% of respondents (from over 2,000 senior HR and business executives) "were satisfied with the degree of accountability demonstrated by their leaders."[9] Only 27% of them believed they had a strong leadership culture in their companies, and only 20% thought their companies had the courage to address mediocre leadership.[10]

Molinaro offers several reasons for these results, including the fact that we have over-relied on the "Heroic Model of Leadership," where "one leader, usually at the top of the organization, has all the answers and can single-handedly lead the way."[11] This is a model that absolutely doesn't work in a complex and uncertain world, specifically because there's no way a leader can know everything necessary in such an environment. Moreover, it means that virtually every corporate action, every decision, must eventually come back to that leader—that one person. There aren't enough hours in the day to allow for this kind of approach to work. Add the explosion of available data to the mix and the Heroic Model fails instantly.

Another flaw that Molinaro found was that companies tend to glorify Charismatic Leaders, turning them into celebrities of a sort. He specifically highlights those who are promoted to the top of their organizations and revered, despite the fact that some act horribly and set a miserable example about what is expected in order to advance professionally. Two examples he cites are Steve Jobs and Uber Technologies' CEO, Travis Kalanick, referring to them as either "brilliant jerks" or, in Jobs' case, a "colossal asshole".[12] The issue again is that this confuses those at the lower levels as to what values are required to succeed in these kinds of companies.

Molinaro also outlines the problem companies exacerbate when they promote "Technical Superstars" into leadership roles. Overnight, the person who was really good at completing one particular task or service is now in charge of everything—and is often ill-equipped to do so. This, in fact, became one of the most important lessons in American business history, when Alfred D. Chandler published his seminal *The Visible Hand* in 1977. This renowned book refocused business from entrepreneurship to management that could sustain a long-term business venture.[13]

Finally, and perhaps most importantly, Molinaro observed that the leadership industry has done more harm than good when it comes to preparing leaders. He notes, "We are dumbing down leadership training and trying to make it too quick and easy to become a good leader." The result is that people with a fancy leadership title don't know what it really takes to be a leader.[14]

Why does any of this matter? The short story is that *our survival in business depends on it.* The business arena is a battlefield, and the way business battles are fought shifts and changes over time. Sticking with yesterday's approach is almost guaranteed to lead to losses tomorrow, and business losses affect lives. The sense of urgency is tremendous. Gary Cokins, in his article on why large, once successful companies fail, notes, "Of the original Standard and Poor's (S&P) 500 list created in 1957, just 74, only 15 percent, are on that list today according to research from Professor Gary Biddle of the University of Hong Kong. Of those 74, only 12 have outperformed the S&P index average. Pretty grim. A few years from now will the sequel to the popular book, 'Good to Great' by Jim Collins reveal the praised companies in the original book as laggards?"[15]

These are the questions we ALL must ask ourselves about the businesses we're in. Will our company be here five or even ten years from now? The assumption that "we've always been in business, and we'll always remain in business" is an unacceptable approach. Just ask the many good people who once worked for TWA, Eastern or Pan Am, Kodak, Sports Authority, Circuit City or Radio Shack—a list, by the way, that's constantly growing. More importantly, is the **industry** we're in still going to be relevant in five or ten years? Think of even the most profitable Blockbuster Video store; it was doomed, no matter what the temporary, local market conditions were. With the rapid and far-reaching transformation of a technology-centric world, it's even questionable how many humans will be required to do once-traditional jobs in the decades to come.

When I first started teaching *The Debrief-Focused Approach*™ to business, I saw it a certain way—the high-performing team approach to improving continuously. The entire fighter pilot method—specifically the way we Plan, Brief, Execute, and Debrief—is rigorously centered on continuous improvement. I know that helping a company to constantly improve is one of the most compelling offers I can personally make. My first-ever client, however, saw it very differently. The principal in a Financial Services firm here in St. Louis, Missouri, saw what I was teaching for what it really is: core training in Accountable Leadership. He asked me to teach *The Debrief-Focused Approach*™ to his entire leadership team so that they could further develop their leadership skills, helping them to better lead their already-successful teams. I realized quickly that he was right. What I took for granted as "the way we did things" as Air Force fighter pilots is actually the way we taught and practiced leadership, and specifically, accountable leadership. It also happened to be the way we practiced agility, resilience and "teaming" in a complex and always-changing environment. I was honored to help train his team in Accountable Leadership. I'm also humbled by the fact that during the first quarter of 2018, his teams hit their marks across-the-board better than at any other time under his leadership. He directly attributed these results to the fact that his teams are debriefing now on a weekly basis, stepping up their collective game and improving the already outstanding performance of an already-winning team.

Loose Lips Sink Ships . . . and So Do Bad Captains!

CAPTAIN Alec Fraser, USN (ret), in his book *Damn the Torpedoes!* notes that the military instills an attitude of "total accountability" in its leadership training approaches, starting at the military academies. He shares his experience as a ship captain and discusses how important this accountability practice is to ensure the safety of his ship. As Fraser explains, "There were no excuses if the mission was not done safely. If a captain thinks someone else can be blamed if something goes wrong, the captain loses the pressure of accountability. When the captain loses that sense of accountability, things go wrong. People get hurt. Ships sink…No excuse means accepting total accountability."[16] Later, he offers a compelling few lines from *The Wall Street Journal* about the collision of two US Navy ships that led to the tragic sinking of one and the loss of many lives: "Responsibility and authority are given only with accountability: 'This accountability is not for the intentions but for the deed. The captain of a ship, like the captain of a state, is given honor and privileges and trust beyond other men. But let him set the wrong course, let him touch ground, let him bring disaster to his ship or to his men, and he must answer for what he has done. He cannot escape.'"[17]

Looking again at the Financial Services firm, the practical challenge the principal was trying to address was the fact that his extremely effective teams were stuck in a rut. They were repeating mistakes, despite being one of the most successful branches in the country. He was frustrated because he heard the same basic story in each quarterly review: his leaders were doing a great job identifying problems and reporting accurately how far short of the mark they were at any given point. But this was where the analysis ended. His team leaders presented these honest results along with justifications for those results, as well as constant affirmations that "next time we'll do it better." He was struggling with the absence of both personal and collective accountability—not because his leaders didn't want to practice it, *but because they never learned how*. Because his leaders didn't understand the various levels of Root Cause analysis, his teams kept making the same mistakes. And because they didn't know how to debrief, his leaders were frustrated and weren't making any headway.

From my perspective as an outsider, the quarterly review sessions were often major sources of frustration for all involved. Despite all members' deep desire to figure out a better way forward, the leadership team was hampered by two complementary issues: 1) their financial success cloaked larger problems; and 2) the teams lacked the tools they needed to break through the barrier to *even better* performance. As is the case in many organizations that do well, it can be difficult to ask, "Why aren't we doing even better?"

It's often hard to get those who are currently achieving success to adopt new approaches and adapt to changing circumstances. It's not uncommon to think, "If it ain't broke, don't fix it". Yet this is part of the root cause as to why 95% of companies that begin another approach to improvement—the "Lean"

Journey—never complete it. Organizational antibodies develop rapidly and multiply quickly, all in an effort to preserve the existing culture.[18] This is also a reason why many successful companies eventually fail.

Consider the American auto industry in the early 1960s. The United States had just emerged from the "golden accident"—a period historians Larry Schweikart and Lynne Doti define as the 15 years following the end of World War II, when America was overwhelmingly dominant in every sector. It was obvious why: much of the world lay in smoking ruins, or had been invaded by communist Russia. Literally, the USA was the only large, developed nation in the world whose homeland was untouched by war. As a result, America accounted for the lion's share of both production *and* consumption. Such a situation had never occurred before in world history. American trade accounted for 15% of the world total, while U.S. manufacturing by some estimates made up around 40% of the world's total.[19]

That's good news, right? Yes, from a certain point of view. Importantly, the American auto industry—along with steel and electronics—assumed that this would be the state of the international markets forever. But Japan and Germany recovered faster than anyone believed possible; and, by the end of the 1960s, competitive Japanese cars and trucks were pouring into the United States and steadily taking market share from the "Big Three." Temporary success had blinded the automobile industry from looking at their current weaknesses.

Why Should We Adopt a New Approach When We're Already Set for Success?

Let's look briefly at the world of sports. Specifically, all sports teams are essentially structured the same way. They each have a head coach and perhaps several assistant coaches. They have players and trainers; they all practice and they work to improve. Yet, some teams consistently perform well, and others stay mired in mediocrity. Some might say it's the "luck of the draw" based on team composition; others might say it's just the nature of life that some teams routinely win and others don't. My contention is that the teams that learn better than the rest and can adapt from this learning are the ones who consistently win.

Take, for example, the New England Patriots. Year after year, this team is in the playoffs; and year after year, they contend and regularly win the Superbowl. The Cleveland Browns are in the same league, and yet they have the exact opposite experience year in and year out; that is, they regularly lose. Yet both teams have the same structure: a head coach, offensive and defensive coaches, special teams and other specialty coaches. They each have strength and conditioning coaches, trainers, nutrition specialists, and the like. Both teams have the same number of players and they both pay their players a LOT of money to play a brutal game. Both teams even have some really good players, selected from a much larger pool of prospects because of their skills, ostensibly because they have what it takes to succeed at the NFL level. In fact, due to their consistently poor performance, almost every year the Browns have a very high draft pick—more than once, the #1 pick in the draft—while the Patriots always draft near the bottom. And yet, both experience vastly different results during the season, every season.

There is no doubt that the Patriots benefit by having one of the best quarterbacks to ever play the game on their team, which makes a huge difference. But in a 2016 USA Today article, former NFL head coach Tony Dungy suggested that the Patriots win because of how their head coach Bill Belichick approaches each game. Dungy explains, "They do a great job of getting the players to adapt and understand that they can do different things. Those kind of situations, they don't bother them. He's the best adjustment coach in football, in adjusting to the strength of his players and masking the weaknesses of their team. It didn't surprise me at all."[20]

Dungy is describing the impact of *proper planning*, and of understanding clearly what each member of the team brings to the table and using that knowledge to their collective advantage. Belichick employs a winning methodology to win. The Browns have everything else the Patriots do—all the positions are filled, they have a good staff, everyone wants to win...but the Browns seemingly don't have access to the key, winning methodology that Belichick employs year in, year out. And this makes all the difference.

The same was true with the legendary UCLA basketball dynasties under coach John Wooden. Years later, his players, including former all-stars such as Bill Walton and Kareem Abdul-Jabbar, recalled how Wooden's preparations resulted in *exactly the same practice every day*, and that he began his teaching process by literally telling them how to tie their shoes.

The point of all this is to say that fielding the top talent, following the same processes, and doing what would *seem* to be the right things doesn't mean that a team is going to win. Far from it, in fact. What actually matters is that the team that wants to win employs the correct soft skills the right way, and then practices, practices, practices, in order to get it right.

Debrief to Win as Part of a Winning Methodology

In order to fully understand how to *Debrief to Win* it helps to briefly explore the entirety of *The Debrief-Focused Approach™*. A complete analysis is too much for this book, so I will cover the broad outlines:

THE DEBRIEF-FOCUSED APPROACH™

We begin *The Debrief-Focused Approach*™ by acknowledging that at the end of our "execution period"—that time when we've actually done something—there is going to be a debrief. It doesn't have to be a long, drawn-out, onerous process. We just need to know that we're going to have an effective debrief. This is critically important, because expecting that everyone will be held accountable for their actions has a *direct impact* on how people behave, and on the decisions they make.

The next phase of the approach is Planning. The planning *process* underpins everything, setting the conditions for team success. Note that the planning process is even more critical than the actual plan. As Geoff Watts, author of *Scrum Mastery* notes, "All plans are arguably wrong anyway because, as soon as they are made, the information used to make them is immediately out of date."[21] While this might sound extreme, I completely agree that the focus of planning should be on the planning process. It's about developing a shared mental model of how a team is going to win, and developing a forecast of the future and how the team can address the challenges this future could present. We have to learn how to plan effectively if we want to execute well.

Mission Briefing—communication of the plan to the team—is equally critical. Briefing the Plan to *all of the members of the team* is essential to inspiring them all to succeed—to do what needs to be done to achieve the objectives, especially when the team's composition changes and when circumstances shift and evolve.

Execution itself is the process of decision-making. There is much here, specifically centered around an approach known in aviation circles as Crew Resource Management or CRM. CRM covers a range of concepts, from Emotional Intelligence to Checklist use, to communication and coordination—all of which warrants a detailed review. And *then*...once all that is done, there's the Debrief—itself a component of CRM.

Just like John Wooden's UCLA practices, every single one of my flying missions followed the exact same approach. Key to this is understanding that the process of planning, executing, then debriefing—*the outcomes of which are integral to the next planning process*—is an operational system that works, and works brilliantly. This approach incorporates critical components of the Toyota Production System, but introduced them well prior to TPS' inception in the 1950's. In fact, the core of this approach has changed little since our nation's first fighter pilots applied this methodology in WWI, and it probably won't change much in the future. The reason being that it's too good a process, and it *works*. This process, coupled with outstanding training, ensures that our nation's high-performing military teams win consistently.

Basic Structure

In *Debrief to Win* I've chosen to write a book on *how* an organization should organize to be able to effectively debrief, and then how to actually *employ* what I call *The Art of the Debrief*—the way high-performing teams functionally debrief. That said, these principles help solve problems at all levels of an organization, as well as in a wide variety of settings. In fact, the utility of this particular tool is extremely far-reaching. In addition, and now for those who study and apply complexity science to their work, this approach works extremely well in the Complicated Domain, but also has applicability in the Complex Domain, for those who follow the work of Snowden and Boone.[22] The bottom line is that *The Debrief-Focused Approach*™ is used to build teams and to build teams of teams, or networks of teams. This approach helps teams to be the absolute best they can be. Central to this approach is the formal Debrief, which is our focus. Those who choose to employ the Debrief regularly choose to learn how to win consistently.

Not Every Organization Can *Debrief to Win*

It's critical to know that not every organization can apply the approach I'm teaching here. In fact, only those companies and organizations that **actually embrace and practice Integrity** can expect to employ this approach with any hope for success. It has become absolutely clear that not every organization actually does this, which means that not every organization is able to *Debrief to Win*. Integrity is a word that gets batted around a great deal, and I think it's important we agree on a definition, as well as to what it means in the context of this book. According to the brilliant author C.S. Lewis, "Integrity is doing the right thing, even when no one is watching." Note that there is no qualifier here that suggests this only applies at work.

Implicit is that there is no boundary to where one always does the right thing. The manifestation of integrity, at least from my perspective as a former leader of a high-performing team, is expressed as follows:

▶ We won't rest until we accomplish our mission. Most importantly, we won't feel satisfied unless we accomplish our mission in accordance with our values;

▶ We aim for excellence in everything we do;

▶ We value the truth above all else, even when it is painful.

With this as our foundation, let's learn how to *Debrief to Win*!

PART ONE
FOUNDATIONS

PRE-BRIEF

"

KNOWING IS NOT ENOUGH;
WE MUST APPLY.
WISHING IS NOT ENOUGH;
WE MUST DO.

Johann Wolfgang Von Goethe

The Extremely-Close Pass

Let's turn briefly to 2003 and a mission I flew as a squadron Weapons Officer—the chief Instructor Pilot in a fighter organization—about a year after I graduated from the USAF Weapons School. My wingman and I were roughly 100 miles out over the Atlantic Ocean, flying a "Basic Fighter Maneuvers" mission, a profile that might be more familiar to you as "dogfighting". The dogfight is a one vs. one mission where the object is to kill the enemy without being shot down. The specific type of "dogfight" we were practicing was one where we started off around 4-5 miles away from each other. At my command, we would simulate having just seen the other, transitioning immediately into a head-on attack. This was followed by high-energy, high-stress maneuvering to get into a suitable firing position on the other aircraft.

The first objective is to learn to position the jet properly for the point at which the aircraft pass each another. The next objective is to transition rapidly into a position to employ weapons to "win" the engagement. Air Force Training Rules—one of the many guidelines to which we adhere to when flying—stipulate that F-15s should pass no closer than 500 feet from one another. When you consider the speeds at which we were traveling (each at almost 600 mph), our combined velocity was roughly 1.5 times the speed of sound. This means that from five miles to where we ended up passing, we didn't have much time to get things right: less than 20 seconds in total.

Mistake #1

On this particular afternoon, every time I pointed my jet at a particular point in space, my opponent pointed his jet at the same. I would then point somewhere else, always striving for the minimum-required spacing (designed for safety)...and he would "mirror" me exactly. It looked from my perspective as if I were flying into my reflection. We went through several of these iterations before it struck me that we were clearly going to hit one another! As I violently pulled on the stick to maneuver my airplane in a last-ditch effort to avoid the inevitable collision, time slowed down. Our airplanes passed mere *feet* from one another. And as the belly of his airplane passed over my cockpit, I could clearly and distinctly make out each individual screw, each individual fastener on the belly of his machine. It was an otherworldly experience, and not one I ever wanted to repeat.

Amazingly, stunningly, shockingly...we did not hit. Once I had a chance to look back and determine that my tails (the tallest part of my airplane and most likely to be shaved off on this kind of a pass) were still connected and that my airplane hadn't been over-stressed to the point of not being able to fly any longer, I called for us to stop fighting (a "Knock-it-Off" in flying parlance). I commanded that we turn off our combat-related systems, rejoin together as a formation, and return home. There was absolutely no point in continuing to train. We needed to immediately determine how things had gone from great to horrible in such a short period of time. In other words, we needed to return to the squadron and debrief this specific engagement immediately.

Once we were safely back on the ground, my wingman came up and apologized. He felt horrible about what had transpired and took responsibility for it. My response was that while I absolutely appreciated his sentiment (he was an outstanding gentleman), I definitely did not want or need an apology. I also told him that he had more at stake in the event of an accident as he was married and had children. On my side, it was just me and my fear of sharks.

One quick aside: this brief story highlights the great quality of the character of the men and women who serve in the Armed Forces; this gentleman felt that he made a mistake and his first action was to apologize, even before we explored the facts. This is the nature of the people who serve—they own their actions and they take responsibility for their decisions.

Understanding Mistake #1

Our immediate concern was to determine the Root Cause— the determination of fault, the ultimate answer to the question "Why did this occur?" That is, we needed to determine why we didn't maintain the safe minimum spacing that we had achieved on so many other missions, on so many other days, across our collective careers. We needed our tried and tested debrief methodology to figure out how to never make that mistake again.

We spent time reconstructing the facts of that part of the mission and uncovering our Fundamental Question and potential answers. We quickly determined that the Root Cause of our near-miss was that my opponent was overly focused on beating me. Plain and simple, he wanted to beat his Weapons Officer so badly that *he lost focus on the real priority for that portion of a complex mission, which was to play his part in maintaining safe separation from me.* His aggressiveness and associated game plan was appropriate, to a point; his plan was to mimic my every move, essentially mirroring me up until the point where our airplanes merged. But he became so fixated on following his plan that he lost all sense of timing and, importantly, the understanding of our relative positions. His micro-focus on only one part of a rapidly-moving and changing mission almost cost us our lives.

We quickly established that the fix—the way he would avoid making this same mistake again—was to modify his decision-making approach while airborne. He would focus specifically on tempering his aggressiveness based on the phase of flight he was in. On a practical level, this meant he would prioritize the Training Rules (the 500-foot separation) when approaching another aircraft. Armed with this knowledge, absolutely a very clear re-affirmation of something we both already knew, both he and I were better equipped to go forth and conquer the next time out.

How We Didn't Let Mistake #1 Become Mistake #2

Now, imagine what might have happened if we didn't step back and assess our situation after the near-miss. Imagine if we set up another fight just like this one and, on the next engagement, he pointed at me just a split-second longer, based on an unchanged and still intense desire to beat me. Imagine if I had made the same mistake. All it would have taken for us to have had a mid-air collision was probably just a split-second more hesitation on either of our parts, and both of our lives would have been forever impacted in a really terrifying way.

Among the several key take-aways from that day is the fact that we made the correct decision to stop fighting, go home and analyze how we got into that tough position. Next, we both walked away from the debrief with a crystal-clear understanding of how to succeed the next time we found ourselves in those circumstances. We also walked out of that debrief confident that neither of us would ever repeat that mistake —there's something about being scared to death that makes a lasting impression on a person. And, as mentioned, my wingman won by immediately owning up to his mistake and absolutely embracing the need to make the necessary changes in his aggressiveness going forward.

> **WE BOTH WALKED OUT OF THAT ROOM CONFIDENT THAT WE HAD DEBRIEFED TO WIN THE NEXT TIME WE BOTH WENT BACK UP TO FLY**

Without this debrief, my wingman's competitive nature could have gotten the better of him. Instead, he implemented the changes we discussed, went on to enjoy a brilliant flying career, and retired with honor. Most importantly, we both walked out of that room confident that we had debriefed to win the next time we both went back up to fly.

What Allowed Us to Quickly Learn and Improve

In our organization, we knew that every mission ended in a debrief. We also knew that if anything escalated from the usual level of danger to something new and different while flying our mission, our best and only approach was to come home and debrief *as soon as possible*. This attitude came from the culture in which we operated and was embedded in the processes we employed daily. It was ingrained in us from the start of our training, and was reinforced by successive waves of leadership and through continuation training throughout our careers. There were no shortcuts to this approach, and every single member of the fighter pilot community embraced this as the way we did our business. We never questioned it, because it was so deeply entrenched. More importantly, we embraced it because of the tremendous value we gained from the approach.

There's a lesson here for every organization that wants to succeed. When you structure yourself appropriately, build good habits by being disciplined and following through with the process—even when it's hard to do—you'll achieve more than you think possible.

CHAPTER 1

WHAT IS A DEBRIEF?

YOU MUST NEVER CONFUSE FAITH THAT
YOU WILL PREVAIL IN THE END—WHICH
YOU CAN NEVER AFFORD TO LOSE—WITH
THE DISCIPLINE TO CONFRONT THE
MOST BRUTAL FACTS OF YOUR CURRENT
REALITY, WHATEVER THEY MIGHT BE.

Admiral Jim Stockdale

*Highest-ranking US POW in Vietnam, Medal of Honor
Winner, as quoted in "Good to Great"*

Webster's Collegiate College Dictionary defines "debrief" as: "to interrogate (as a pilot), usu. upon return (as from a mission) in order to obtain useful information.[23] While I don't find this definition especially satisfying ("useful information" is a poor description of what we're really obtaining), it is important to note that Webster's picks aviation as its basis for defining the term. This is not to suggest that debriefs are exclusive to aviation; different communities use different terms to describe the same basic process. "After-Action Review" is the term used in the Army, whereas the Marine Corps tends to use "Lessons Learned Reports" or a related variant. In the software development world, the term is "Retrospectives" and there's an entire industry dedicated to facilitating this form of debrief. But pilots have been debriefing their missions as long as they've been flying, and fighter pilot debriefs—the kind I'll be describing—derive from a distinguished and lengthy heritage.

Origins

Fighter pilot debriefs have been around since at least World War I. In a U.S. Army Command and General Staff College paper titled "Armed for Success: External Factors of the World War I Aces" by Maj John P.H. Rayder, the author examines the experience of Edward Mannock. Mannock was "An exceptional leader" who "conducted thorough briefs and debriefs-stressing formation, aggressiveness and tactical judgment" while training the members of his flight.[24] More broadly, Rayder notes that late in WWI, "specialized pilot training was established at the institutional level, taking form in an equivalent of today's fighter weapons schools. Prior to this the responsibility for pilot training rested solely upon individuals within the fighting units. It was this training opportunity at the front that the aces influenced." Furthermore, "This training consisted of specified conditions which included preflight briefs, postflight debriefs and dedicated analysis and understanding of the tactics employed."[25] Finally, this brief-debrief process was used by both sides. Rayder notes that, "Early German squadron-level training programs of detailed preflight briefs, post flight debriefs, and tactics analysis laid the foundation for the air combat success of several German pilots…The Germans were in command of air combat in early 1917 as a result of their training and the superiority of the Albatros [sic] fighter."[26]

> ORGANIZATIONS THAT EMPLOY DEBRIEFS ARE THOSE THAT HARBOR AN INTENSE DESIRE TO WIN

The one common thread between the fighter debriefs that started in WWI, and the various forms of debriefs previously listed is the nature of the organization that chose to use this tool. Organizations that employ debriefs are those that harbor an intense desire to win. Winning teams use debriefs as a regular, standard practice. Some examples of these types of teams include U.S. Navy SEALS, Army Rangers and the Special

Operations Community in general. Sports teams, both professional and amateur, use a version as well. For example, in 2011 the New York Giants held a debrief every 1-2 days after their games to understand what worked and what didn't.[27] Incidentally, that was the year they went on to win the Superbowl.

Many businesses understand this fact, and many of them are attempting to use this capability to their advantage. In his book, *Good to Great*, author Jim Collins notes that the companies that "Conduct autopsies, without blame" have developed cultures where the "truth is heard". Those autopsies are a form of debrief. Collins goes on to note that, "Leadership does not begin just with vision. It begins with getting people to confront the brutal facts and to act on the implications...One of the primary ways to de-motivate people is to ignore the brutal facts of reality."[28]

Debriefs start with the brutal facts and use these to determine whether or not the job was done correctly. Not doing so is dangerous; in his book *Project Retrospectives*, Norman Kerth suggests, "By avoiding a review of a failed project, the community loses a valuable opportunity to learn from its experience, possibly leaving the door open for the same kind of failure to happen again."[29]

In their best-selling book *Extreme Ownership*, popular speakers and leadership trainers Jocko Willink and Leif Babin make frequent reference to the constancy of their post-mission debriefs. They specifically note, "The best SEAL units, after each combat operation, conduct what we called a 'post-operational debrief.' No matter how exhausted from an operation or how busy planning for the next mission, time is made for this debrief because lives and future mission success depend on it. A post-operational debrief examines all phases of an operation from planning through execution, in a concise format. It addresses the following for the combat mission just completed: What went right? What went wrong? How can we adapt our tactics to make us even more effective and increase our advantage over the enemy? Such self-examination allows SEAL units to reevaluate, enhance, and refine what worked and what didn't so that they can constantly improve. It is critical for the success of any team in any business to do the same and implement those changes into their future plans so that they don't repeat the same mistakes."[30]

There are many approaches to the general process of debriefing, and each has its defined purpose. Several forms of debriefs that stand out include Process-sequential (strong overlap with teaching); Psychological (typically used post-trauma); Agile Retrospectives (stemming from a software development focus); Unstructured (ad hoc, the most common type in use); and Objectives-focused / methodology-based. It is useful to briefly review these types:

*The **Process-Sequential Debrief** is my term for the type of debrief we use in Air Force pilot training. It's built on the concept that every part of every mission is evaluated postflight. We judge the various components of the mission against a set of standards, and assign grades for each phase of flight and mission element. By following the flow of the debrief/ grade sheet, the instructor pilot is able to instruct the student on any deviations from standards. The process for debriefing a roughly one-hour mission lasts roughly one hour. The take-away from this type of debrief is both an understanding of how to correct any mistakes moving forward, as well as an over-all grade that helps determine student progression and overall standing. This kind of debrief is especially effective in a one-on-one setting centered in an academic or learning context.

*The **Psychological Debrief** is an important tool, especially following traumatic experiences. A lot of work was conducted in this field in World War II, to help those who had witnessed and experienced horrors in the execution of that war. My own father was a facilitator of one of these types of debriefs, as he was assigned the several months-long task of debriefing a returning Prisoner of War from Vietnam. A lot of what my father did was open the floodgates for horrible memories of the torture and trauma experienced by this individual at the hands of his captors. Today, Police departments use these types of de-briefs to work with people who have been traumatized due to crime, and there are a variety of ways in which this version of the debrief can be effectively harnessed to tremendous benefit.

*The **Agile Retrospective** offers many useful techniques to help software designers figure out how to build software better. This community relies heavily on the use of games to help do things like build psychological safety, as well as to spur conversation and communication among members of the design team. This game-centric approach preferred by the Retrospective facilitator offers much in terms of setting the conditions for debrief success, especially early on in the adoption process. Because of its utility in the software engineering world, the process has been transferred into other domains that seek a workable debriefing methodology. One of the biggest problems with applying Retrospectives in non-software domains is the non-repeatability of this methodology; each Retrospective Facilitator comes armed with a toolkit of games and approaches to spur learning, any of which he or she might employ to spark discussion and arrive at conclusions. Since the choice of games is an independent decision of the Facilitator, and since this methodology isn't centered on evaluating performance against a set standard, the results can and do vary. In addition, the accuracy of the results achieved by this means is also highly variable, leading to a widely varying level of quality. Much of the "success" of this approach is tied to the skill of the Facilitator who is, by definition, someone that is brought in from outside the team to guide it—often over the course of many days—to produce conclusions. Later, we'll discuss the implications of conducting debriefs that lead to faulty conclusions; know that Agile Retrospectives contain a large margin of error in their outcomes. Ultimately, the inefficiency of this approach, its reliance on the guidance of an outside Facilitator and the fact that the results can vary so wildly, are all challenges in adapting it to debriefing outside of the field for which it was originally designed. The good news is that these kinds of debriefs are a great starting point, and can help accelerate an organization's adoption of fighter pilot debriefs.

*The **Unstructured Debrief** is one where a group organizes to review a process, an event, a planning cycle etc., but lacks a defined methodology. They discuss areas of concern and raise various points, but there is no real ability to repeat the process per-se—because there is no real process to begin with. It's an ad-hoc effort meant to help arrive at worthwhile conclusions. As such, good outcomes are entirely possible, but so are faulty ones. Strong personalities tend to dominate these kinds of debriefs, and those who can't or won't dominate often go unheard. The real problem with this approach is that those who go unheard can't provide their perspectives of what took place, which means that the true picture of what actually happened never emerges. An unstructured debrief may actually reinforce those "golden accident" tendencies in successful organizations that nevertheless have serious problems. People may believe that an unstructured debrief led to positive outcomes, but the absence of methodology means that what looks good may really be faulty conclusions. We'll cover an example of one of these and the associated outcome in Chapter 6.

*The **Objectives-Focused /Methodology-Based Debrief** is the type of debrief we're going to focus on throughout this book. This is the debrief of choice for the fighter pilot—the way the High-Reliability Organization known as the American fighter squadron operates day-in, day-out, across the entire globe. This approach works because it's based on science. It is a repeatable methodology that can be applied in a wide range of contexts. It's centered on task accomplishment and can be used in everything from high-complexity combat missions to Human Resource concerns, from risk mitigation to helping a team build resilience. The *context* of the debrief determines the overall approach as well as the degree of specificity or detail arrived at. This, in-turn, determines the amount of time and degree of sophistication spent on the process itself. For example, a debrief addressing why a life was lost in an aircraft accident will be much more comprehensive than one dealing with why the team successfully achieved its objectives. The Objectives-Focused/Methodology-Based debrief is a variation of the "Task-Oriented Debriefing" outlined by Dr. Arieh Shalev in his report titled, "Historical Group Debriefing Following Combat,"[31] and traces its roots to the beginning of fighter aviation in the early 1900's. That said, and regardless of the context, all fighter pilot debriefs serve the same overall purpose: *to understand the absolute truth of what happened so as to evaluate performance and*

> A DEBRIEF IS THE PROCESS OF CONSTRUCTIVELY EVALUATING THE QUALITY OF THE DECISIONS EVERYONE ON THE TEAM MADE FROM PLANNING THROUGH EXECUTION, IN RELATION TO THE OBJECTIVES THE TEAM SET OUT TO ACHIEVE

drive future improvement. This specific process drives the development of a high-performance culture, which helps fighter squadrons consistently win in the toughest of environments—the high-speed, high-G force, high-complexity environment of air-to-air combat. Armed with an ability to employ this methodology, every leader, at every level, in any organization will be capable of driving massive process improvement.

Lastly, it's critical to note that debriefing is not a fad, trend, or pseudo-science. The fighter pilot debrief methodology is a battle-tested process that nurtures constant improvement in individuals and organizations. At its core it supports a deep understanding of human psychology and the study of human interactions. It is the one critical element necessary for High-Performing Teams to function correctly. It is also the way that you can change organizational culture for the better.

My Definition of a Debrief

A debrief is the process of constructively evaluating the quality of the decisions everyone on the team made from planning through execution, in relation to the objectives the team set out to achieve. Central to a properly-run debrief is the actual practice of Accountable Leadership. It's an accountability practice because everyone on the team, both follower and leader alike, will be evaluated on the quality of the decisions they made from planning through execution. It's a leadership skill because someone has to be in charge and actually lead. A debrief is a process that can, because of the nature of the human interactions involved, get intense and touchy.

Critically, a debrief is **not** a gruesome sport or a place of blame or shame. Quite the opposite, in fact—the debrief is **where we celebrate our victories** as well as **learn from our failures**. We do this in order to build cohesive teams and improve moving forward. A debrief properly run is an affirming, positive experience. It is also where we build future leaders.

The whole point of this accountability process and leading effectively is the development of teams that practice great Teamwork, which is separate and distinct from Taskwork.[32] To be clear, Taskwork is the "doing of things," the part that's relatively easy and can often be done by individuals operating by themselves, even if they're formally part of a team. Teamwork, on the other hand, is the piece that must be present for a group of people to actually function as a team. The debrief facilitates turning what Dr. Eduardo Salas refers to as "Teams of Experts into Expert Teams".[33] It is a team intervention event, designed to address the challenges human beings have in working together, in making decisions supportive of group goals, and overcoming objections. Leaders should have a clear "understanding of what drives effective teamwork, such as appropriate communications, backup behavior, role clarity, and shared mental models." [34] Good teamwork depends on quality debriefs.

Besides Accountable Leadership, What Else Can You Gain from a Good Debrief?

To answer this question, I'll first borrow from the world of Agile Retrospectives, the software development debrief process. I do so because I think the following does a very nice job of capturing the core "whys" for those who aren't familiar with the need for effective debriefs. Among the many reasons to conduct a debrief is the fact that debriefs allow teams and individuals 1) To learn and improve rapidly without blame or shame; 2) To celebrate success; and 3) To build a tribe and pass along tradition.[35]

The first point is absolutely key. As teams, we must learn to fail forward, to accept the fact that we can't be our best if we don't push the envelope and miss the mark at times. Doing so in an objective way, one where we "focus on the behaviour [sic] and not the individual(s)"[36] is essential to building what we'll soon discover to be psychological safety. The key standard underlying this approach is that we're not doing anything illegal, immoral, or uncalled for. Any mistakes we make are exactly that: mistakes made while trying to do our best. Daniel Burrus, author of *The Anticipatory Organization*, highlights the importance of organizations learning to "fail fast". Specifically, "Not only does Failing Fast move you past the emotions and dynamics of failing, it helps you to learn faster. In other words, you interpret what happened, share what you've learned from the mistake, and move forward, rather than pointlessly wallowing in it." Furthermore, "If you don't share what you learn when you fail, you're effectively allowing someone else to replicate the same mis-step. To make the most of the value of failing, let those around you in on what you've learned. The faster you fail, the faster you learn!"[37] We see this in Major League Baseball, where players review their swings immediately after their at-bats or between innings, based on video taken in real-time.

The second point is probably one that many organizations struggle with quite a bit: celebrating success on an individual level. There are plenty of reasons for this. Chief among these is that fact that in a time-constrained environment, it's extremely easy to focus on those things that didn't go well while overlooking those that did. Often, team members struggle with the sense that they aren't appreciated for the good that they've done. Debriefs actually help address the basic human need for affirmation and positive recognition. Specifically, the debrief provides an outstanding, regular forum in which leaders get to highlight their teams as a whole, as well as individual team members, for the great work that was done. In addition, the Objectives-Focused/Methodology-Based Debrief ensures that everyone present understands not only *how* but *why* the great work that was done achieved success. This methodology validates and verifies the activities that the leader can then praise, making the process objective. It also offers an opportunity for other members of the team to learn how they can replicate the success being highlighted. In other words, everyone gets to win.

I look at the third point—building a tribe—as defining our culture, which is the experience I had practicing this approach over my Air Force career. Author Chris Fussell, in his book *One Mission: How Leaders Build a Team of Teams*, notes,

"Because members usually do not choose which team would be the best culture fit for them, instead being assigned to a team, the individual adapts to the culture of the tribe."[38] While Chris is referring to Navy SEALS, the same applies to the way fighter pilots arrive in their squadrons—mostly by selection, not by choice. Debriefs help these new arrivals understand and adapt to the culture, which is critically important when it comes to building high-performing teams. New members must quickly learn and embrace the culture for the team to remain high-performing throughout disruption and change. The debrief is the absolute best way to ensure this happens.

But What's the Real Bonus from Implementing Good Debriefs?

Simply put, learning how to debrief to win gives you the ability to move into the realm of anticipatory thinking, a framework that allows companies and organizations to thrive in the midst of disruption. Says Daniel Burrus, "Organizations of all types and sizes have traditionally relied on their ability to react as quickly as possible to shifting challenges, the demands of the marketplace, and other types of disruptions. That's often referred to as agility. Being agile is very important, but it is simply no longer good enough. We are living in an era of increasing disruption—not simple change, but outright transformational change. Revolutionary technology and business concepts are rendering traditional systems and modes of thinking less relevant and even obsolete at an increasing pace."

The debrief serves as a means of rapidly correcting and then feeding these corrections into the next phase of planning. *In an anticipatory organization, planning is always on-going.* Results are constantly scrutinized, and plans are adapted and changed to meet emerging needs. Most importantly, plans are adjusted to anticipate disruptions, allowing anticipatory organizations to thrive where non-anticipatory organizations find themselves struggling just to hang on.

How Does Your Company Debrief?

In my time working as a professional business consultant and leadership trainer, I've been fortunate to have worked with successful businesspeople and other professionals who uniformly acknowledge the tremendous need for good debriefs. Initially, some of these business veterans believe that they already employ something similar in their organizations. However, when faced with a few pointed questions, it almost always becomes immediately clear that the expectations of what determines the quality of a debrief vary wildly. In the end, there's often a tremendous gap between where a company is right now in employing this tool, and where it is that they could—and should—be. This stems from the fact that there is currently very little training available on how to properly employ debriefs in a business setting. There's more written about its utility than on how to do it effectively and properly, which presents a problem.

It is abundantly clear that some of our sharpest organizations are trapped, executing what we'll come to know as

"Level 1" debriefs, where they should be at "Level 3" (we'll define these levels shortly). A Level 1 debrief translates to error identification and explanation, demonstrated in statements such as:

> *"We missed the mark this month because Sam was out sick for two weeks. We'll do better next month because Sam is feeling better now."*

While this type of answer identifies both an error and a potential answer to why that error happened, it is ***entirely insufficient*** for an organization that wants to win. It pointedly fails to explain why the success of the organization is dependent on "Sam." We'll discover later the difference that Levels 2 and 3 debriefs bring to this discussion, tying these qualities to the Level 5 leadership traits Jim Collins shares in his outstanding book *Good to Great*.

The Need for a Massive Sense of Urgency

What I've ultimately found is that moderately-sized Fortune 500 companies are sometimes tragically unprepared for the form of combat in which they are currently engaged. Their sights are set too low; they really don't plan well, and they're too often satisfied with "keeping the good thing going," which is whatever success it is they enjoy today. Remember, it was specifically this kind of thinking that destroyed the American auto and steel industries. Most critically, they lack the sense of urgency that comes with a combat mindset.[39] "Business is only business," they say to me. They share that they don't have the pressure of flying a high-performance aircraft in harm's way, which means that they feel they can afford to make mistakes and take unnecessary risks. I completely disagree.

I admittedly come from a completely different world— one where the stakes are incredibly high and where the price of failure is absolutely unacceptable. I've lost friends who have paid the ultimate price and I struggle with those losses. Yet I disagree with those who say business isn't the same as combat, because people's lives and fortunes are absolutely at stake in business. Whether it's the owner, the shareholders, *the workers themselves*, or the countless others affected by a given company's success or failure, business is a dangerous game in which there are winners and losers. I can't bear to see good teams lose—and I see losses happening around me in business every day. These losses stem from the way businesses operate, and they are tolerated because many people truly don't sense the urgency at hand—that is, until it is too late. By the time they appreciate the position they're in, the company has laid off a bunch of workers, closed several locations, stopped promotions, eliminated raises and incentives, and seen tensions mount daily. These are companies where leaders are unable to provide appropriate, usable, productive feedback. They don't know how to grow leaders because they don't practice sound leadership. And thus, the cycle perpetuates itself.

CONCLUSION

There are many different forms of debrief. The one outlined in *Debrief to Win* is the one fighter pilots have been practicing since WWI. What's interesting is that organizations don't know what they don't know—even those who believe they currently debrief well have much to learn. What's just as important is that there's a tremendous urgency for organizations to do so, given the disruptions taking place in the marketplace today. In the next chapter we'll discuss the *culture* and *values* an organization must embrace and actually live in order to be able to debrief properly.

SUMMARY

▶ Debriefs have been used effectively by fighter pilots since World War I.

▶ There are many forms of debriefs; this book is focused on the Objectives-Focused/Methodology-Based Debrief.

▶ A debrief is the process of constructively evaluating the quality of the decisions everyone on the team made from planning through execution, in relation to the objectives the team set out to achieve.Debriefing properly—specifically without blame orshame—has many benefits, to include developing anticipatory organizations.

▶ Organizations don't know what they don't know; even those that currently practice debriefing have much to learn, because there is currently is very little training available on how to do it correctly.

CHAPTER 2

CULTURAL FOUNDATIONS

IF YOU DON'T KNOW WHERE YOU'RE
GOING, ANY ROAD WILL TAKE YOU THERE

Chet Richards

Certain to Win

A Little Insight into How Fighter Pilots Use Stories to Improve

It's Friday afternoon at 4:27 PM. The setting is the Squadron Bar, physically located within the fighter squadron building. The lights are low, flight suits are worn out of regulation—

this is intentional. Some people are smoking cigars, and almost everyone has a frothy mug of beer or beverage of their choice. The mugs proudly reveal pilot callsigns as well as the squadron's patch (for those pilots who are already "named"). Guests of the bar and "unnamed" members of the squadron (pilots who are too new to have yet earned a callsign) make use of mugs set aside for those who aren't fully-vested members of the team.

With a rap of the gavel, "The Mayor"—one of the junior pilots selected for his outstanding sense of humor, ability to control the mob, and general Situational Awareness—yells the word "Hack," short for "Time Hack" (the official decree of what time it is, designed for time synchronization prior to a mission). "Roll Call" comes to order. The next thing The Mayor always does is call out the names of everyone assigned and attached to the squadron, and keeps tabs on who is there and who isn't (Roll Call attendance is voluntary). Those who aren't and who haven't legitimately "called-in" with excusable alibies (The Mayor is the final arbiter of all alibis) are assessed appropriate fines for their non-presence.

Thus begins the informal accountability process, as well as the deepening of the squadron's culture. This is the "ying" to the "yang" of the formal mission debriefs that took place throughout the week. Often some pilots are still debriefing their Friday missions despite the fact that Roll Call is underway. In fact, these pilots may still be debriefing their missions well into the night while the rest of the squadron is celebrating another successful week of flying. This "ying" serves as the chance to build rapport with teammates. Critically, it also provides an opportunity to cover the lessons of the week in an informal setting.

Much learning occurs both during and after Roll Call, amidst the stories, the songs, and the revelry. The stories are always the best part, largely because the only requirement is that the story be a mere 10% true. You can only imagine how this plays out. The bottom line is that if you, say, accidentally taxied (drove) your jet down the wrong taxiway on Monday, Friday's story surely becomes 10 times worse, full of all sorts of hilarious additions. The primary goal of telling the story, of course, is to bring the squadron to stitches. The secondary effect of these stories is that they reinforce, always in an intentionally funny way, the standards that the team expects every one of its members to uphold. Violations of the standards are simply not tolerated.

The penalties that "Mr. Mayor" assigns can be entertaining. For instance, the pilot who made a major, if unintentional, mistake that week might be punished by having to wear a 1920's-era football helmet for the rest of the evening. Someone else may be threatened with an "Emergency Re-Naming" (a threat of getting a new callsign that highlights the mistake that occurred). I recall a situation where a young pilot accidentally rolled his jet off the runway and into the grass. The jet's wheels dug into the soil and the aircraft came to a jarring and uncomfortable stop in a place it clearly didn't belong. That pilot was actually subject to a re-naming, an event that happens very rarely in the F-15 world. His callsign was changed from what it originally was to "Tractor."

This seemed at the time to be highly-appropriate justice, as well as a hilarious way to highlight a point.

At the same time, the assembled pilots were also always open and sympathetic to demonstrations of humility and personal acceptance of responsibility. If you over-G'd (over-stressed) your aircraft while maneuvering in flight—something we could easily do in the F-15—the impact was that the jet probably wasn't available to fly for some time as it went through a rigorous set of safety inspections. The maintenance professional assigned to that airplane now had additional, demanding work to do. Our team had one less available aircraft to fly, which might impact training. Mind you, it is far too easy to over-stress the airplane, and we're always pushing the limits of performance while airborne. At the same time, we want people to get close to over-stressing, without crossing the line. Maneuvering to the point of the "over-G" wasn't an intentional act, and every pilot could easily justify having done so as part of the job. That said, we also wanted to teach ourselves to fly to the point just shy of the "over-G", maximizing performance while not impacting either maintenance or the members of the squadron. The squadron culture demanded perfection, and would not tolerate an infraction.

In this case, the expectation was that the pilot in question *at a minimum,* offer libations both to his crew chief, and the squadron. These libations were offered as humble recognition of a mistake made, a token of contrition, and a way to buy back into the team's good graces. Such gestures were uniformly accepted, and the pilot was always "cleared" by the squadron. The same offer was always acceptable for any other violations of our norms. Thus, we established that our team understood we all make mistakes—we just expected our teammates to own up to their mistakes. It was as simple as that.

It was always interesting to me that rank was not usually a major issue at Roll Call. The majority of the time, the most senior officers were not assigned egregious punishments; but they were handed out from time to time, depending on the gravity of the mistake. And the best of the senior officers came armed with libations and gifts to the bar, thereby solidifying themselves as team players, and showing that they, too, had once been young fighter pilots and understood the process.

Most importantly, it was this setting that really opened people up to the fighter pilot culture, right from the beginning of their fighter pilot careers. And the young pilots responded. The use of stories and humor to highlight issues from the week that the tribe didn't want to see repeated was a way of holding ourselves collectively accountable. It was done in a way that was forward-looking ("We're not going to repeat these mistakes"), as opposed to backward-looking ("This person is a bad pilot"). The offering to the bar was a public acknowledgement that a member of the team let the whole team down and felt bad about it. The literal paying of a price was symbolic of wanting to repay the team for the poor public display of skills, capability and standards' adherence. Critically, this open acknowledgment of error, willingness to discuss it in front of leadership, and the leadership's participation in the process where required all helped set the conditions that, on Monday, would be necessary for continued effective debriefs.

So How Does Any of This Apply to Your Company?

These techniques are evidence of but one of the ways in which we instill Psychological Safety, something we'll talk about shortly, in our squadrons. The strong reliance on humor provides a powerful way to discuss mistakes that had the potential to be deadly. Humor helped us address the fact that the job was exceedingly dangerous, and helped us re-emphasize points that demanded our attention. Because we could laugh about it, we knew we were going to be OK. Critically, this approach is in no way exclusive to fighter squadrons.

I worked with a really wonderful company in South Carolina that used the same basic approach in their workplace. They have a bar on their second floor, and team members who have been employed for three months or more "earn" a personal mug with their name etched on the side. These new employees were vested to some small degree and have achieved the status necessary to become part of that company's "tribe." This corporate bar is the setting for conversations of a more light-hearted nature and the effect is powerful. People who work here count down the days until Monday, seemingly because they really enjoy coming to work.

Remove the bar from the equation and substitute the formal "Mayor-led" and humor-centric process with one of absolute humility, and we see the way that another outstanding company I've been privileged to spend time with operates. Instead of the stories that are only 10% true, this company starts off their meetings by having every participant, including their most senior leaders (CEO, COO and CFO included), share both a personal and a professional challenge they're dealing with. These stories are sometimes intense, and always brutally honest. It's not uncommon for tears to be shed, and truths are set forth that would surprise an outside observer. People who work here are open, honest and share a degree of trust I haven't seen elsewhere outside of the military. This company has truly figured out how to build teams by employing Psychological Safety as the powerful tool it can and must be.

Psychological Safety and a Team-Centric Approach

So—what exactly *is* Psychological Safety? According to Amy C. Edmondson, Novartis Professor of Leadership and Management at the Harvard Business School, and noted thought leader in this field, Psychological Safety describes "a climate in which people are comfortable being (and expressing) themselves."[42] Laura Delizonna, Stanford University instructor and founder of ChoosingHappiness.com notes, "Studies show that psychological safety allows for moderate risk-taking, speaking your mind, creativity, and sticking your neck out without fear of having it cut off —just the types of behavior that lead to market breakthroughs."[43] At its core, it's about trust, without which there is no team.[44] Delizonna continues, "The brain processes a provocation by a boss, competitive co-worker, or dismissive subordinate as a life-or-death threat. The amygdala, the alarm bell in the brain, ignites the fight-or-flight response, hijacking higher brain centers. This "act first, think later" brain structure shuts down perspective and analytical reasoning. Quite literally, just when we need it most, we lose our minds. While that fight-or-flight reaction may save us in life-or-death situations, it handicaps the strategic thinking needed in today's workplace."[45]

> ❝ PSYCHOLOGICAL SAFETY DESCRIBES "A CLIMATE IN WHICH PEOPLE ARE COMFORTABLE BEING (AND EXPRESSING) THEMSELVES."

Squadron Roll Calls were only one way in which we worked hard to maintain our Psychological Safety, but only one. There is no doubt that the principal way we established Psychological Safety was through the personal example our flight leads demonstrated in our post-mission debriefs every single day. These leaders specifically displayed personal fallibility and admitted their own failures, components of Psychological Safety as outlined in Edmondson's work *Teaming: How organizations learn, innovate, and compete in the knowledge economy.*[46] We'll explore this concept in more detail in Chapter 4, but know that the display of fallibility is the critical ingredient in the maintenance of psychological safety in the fighter squadron. I would argue that it is also what makes our leaders so effective in doing their jobs across the board, even outside of the flying world. As a young pilot, I simply accepted that this is "the way we do it"; upon further reflection, it turns out the Air Force understood the necessity of this approach and ensured we were appropriately equipped for debrief success.

It also turns out that much of why the Air Force does what it does is rooted in science, specifically the science of human interactions. Psychological Safety plays a tremendous role in this, as does the existing squadron culture. During my career, I was fortunate to have been a member of nine flying squadrons, of which six were fighter squadrons. Importantly, each of these squadrons was laser-focused on winning. Each was also centered on doing everything to the best of the team's collective ability. Culture may not be everything to an organization, but it may be the most important "something" to improve on, if we're in the business of developing a culture centered on excellence.

High-Performing Teams and the Centrality of Truth

Kristi Hedges defines a team as, "a group of people who are interdependent in order to accomplish their goals. As Jon R. Katzenback and Douglas K. Smith discussed in their seminal work, *The Discipline of Teams*, 'teams have four elements—common commitment and purpose, performance goals, complementary skills, and mutual accountability.'"[47] This means that being a team is something people have to work at and, to some degree, earn. It's not just a title, and there's more to it than is suggested by an organizational chart.

Based on this definition, lots of groups who think of themselves as teams actually aren't. *Just because smart people come together and do similar tasks in the same space, and just because they might report together on their collective progress, it does not mean they are a team.* For one thing, most groups lack the mutual accountability component that Katzenback and Smith describe. From my vantage point, the accountability process is both the most important and the most challenging element of being on a team. This is specifically where team members are called to take responsibility for the decisions they've made. And the first step of personal responsibility involves acknowledging the truth of whatever happened.

A huge "win" for companies and organizations that implement a debrief-focused model is the adoption of a culture centered on the truth. Jim Collins, in *Good to Great* wrote, "Yes, leadership is about vision. But leadership is equally about creating a climate where the truth is *heard* and the brutal facts confronted. There's a huge difference between the opportunity to 'have your say' and the opportunity to be heard. The good-to-great leaders understood this distinction, creating a culture wherein people had a tremendous opportunity to be heard and, ultimately, for the truth to be heard."[48]

Let me be clear—accountability begins and ends with the *truth* of what happened. The same is true of the debrief. The only way that a person can be accountable for the events that took place, and the only way that a debrief can be effective, is if all participants are focused on *the absolute truth* of what happened throughout the process. Let me also be clear—debriefs can be painful because they require us to be truthful in front of our teammates. This is what makes Psychological Safety so critical. Unless we have it in place and we're consistently working hard to maintain it, the truth will not come out, and the debrief will not be effective. Please keep this in the forefront of your mind as we move forward in this book.

Accountability Starts at the Top

Central to everything I have ever learned about leadership is the fact that leaders lead from the front. Not from the comfort of their office, not from the safety of a rear-echelon or behind the relative "protection" of PowerPoint slides—leaders lead from the front. The goal in the fighter squadron was always to be the leader on night one of the war. That was the ultimate ambition for every self-respecting fighter pilot, and we trained for this possibility throughout our careers. And we enabled people to lead from the front by having them prove that they had what it takes to do so…that they were credible enough to be trusted, and humble enough to admit when they screwed up. The ability to lead from the front is critical in an accountable organization, and the leaders who led on night one— in my experience—were the kinds of leaders who held themselves accountable for their decisions on the battlefield. I was privileged to be raised in an organization that worked in this manner.

Critical to this approach of leading from the front are

followers who strive to become good leaders. In every fighter organization we empower our young wingmen to speak their minds, and to share what they see about the problems we face. This includes calling out senior pilots and officers for mistakes that took place while airborne.

As a young Captain and newly-promoted flight lead, I led a one-star general on a combat sortie over Iraq one sunny afternoon. His stated expectation of my debrief was that I treat him like any other wingman in the squadron. I knew he meant what he said, and I strove to do exactly as requested. At the same time, I acknowledge that we are all human, that we must be tactful in how we debrief senior staff; there really is no such thing as absolutely "nameless and rank-less" in a senior-leader debrief. However, we try. The key here was that the general expected me to do what I was trained to do, and he truly didn't want to be treated differently because of his rank or position. Bear this in mind as we explore this process.

What Enables this Approach? A Values System Centered on Integrity

The only way that our front-line, battle-tested fighter squadrons can operate in the way I've described is that they embrace the required values in their daily lives. I believe that most companies, and certainly the ones with which I've been fortunate to work, both claim to have, and really *want* to practice the values we'll explore. Unfortunately, I've found that many companies fail to live by their professed values, because *they don't live by them on a daily basis.* The values are a desired element, but the daily grind—and how the team adapts to this grind—is the reality of what the company truly values. If we look back at the challenging state of leadership accountability in global enterprise, we see the truth: the values we bring into our companies are typically those we practice at home. Few people are willing to embrace those found on the PowerPoint slide or office bulletin board "just because." According to Harvard Business Review writer John Coleman, "A company's values are its core." That said, values are irrelevant "unless they are enshrined in a company's practices."[49]

> VALUES ARE IRRELEVANT "UNLESS THEY ARE ENSHRINED IN A COMPANY'S PRACTICES."

I propose that the values needed in an organization that aims to practice accountable leadership include, at a minimum: Ethical Behavior, Personal Responsibility, Personal and Professional Growth, Integrity, Service and Excellence. If it sounds like these values come from your company or organization, it's because they do. These are the critical values that enable people on high-performing teams to step forward from their leadership positions and admit failure. These are also the values that, if truly incorporated into the organization's practices, promote an environment where the newest member of the team believes they can speak the truth, without fear of reprisal or punishment.

Chief among these values is Integrity; it's also the value you can most quickly and easily lose, and may never get back. As mentioned at the outset, Integrity is THE fundamental value that underpins everything else. Without it, creating a debrief-centric culture will be impossible.

The Team Has to Believe in the Approach

The need for universal buy-in is relatively obvious; you' won't succeed if only some people play by the rules. The challenge with any business organization, especially today, is that there is constant turnover. How do new people "buy in" to a culture? Even in a fighter squadron, there is constant personnel churn. We're always losing key people and replacing them with new people who often don't have the same qualifications as those they're replacing. Most Active Duty pilots are on a rotation schedule that can be as short as 12 months (sometimes even less) and may only be as long as three years.

In part, dealing with turnover begins with the leadership team. Once they're on-board, the next step is to transmit and reaffirm this fact *regularly* through the debrief. In this way, the debrief ends up being both the desired end and the means of achieving this end. In his book on Lean Transformations, George Koenigsaecker addresses this concept when discussing culture. "An organizational culture is defined by the behaviors or habits of its leaders; in other words, the culture is formed by what these leaders do. 'What they do' is essential to the company's success. When you add lots of these 'what they do's' together, you see the fabric of a new culture."[50] Peter Desloge, CEO of St Louis-based Watlow, expands on this point of seeking global buy-in as he notes, "In the past, senior management had tried to define Watlow's culture by creating value, vision, and mission statements that looked good on the wall, yet never took hold in the organization. We knew that to be successful this time, a completely new approach was needed. This new approach needed to create broad buy-in from our global population, as well as to define the critical values, principles, and behaviors required to ensure Watlow's continued Lean development."[51]

You might be wondering why, in a book about debriefs I'm referring to a book on "Lean Transformations." The simple answer is that both approaches can be difficult to implement because they challenge the status quo. As such, they both require a sincere and complete commitment to adoption as the company's new "Operating System." Because both require changing what people are used to doing, both will encounter significant resistance on implementation. This is why the techniques used to implement one are useful for implementing the other. The good news is that *The Debrief-Focused Approach*™, and its central tenet of the debrief, is easier to adopt than a Lean Transformation because it is designed to be used daily, and in all circumstances, by everyone in the organization.

CONCLUSION

The main thrust of this chapter has been on the *culture* and *values* an organization must embrace and actually live in order to be able to debrief properly. The next chapter will introduce the *processes* that must also be in place to enable successful debriefs. Debriefing in the absence of either of these important components will not be nearly as effective or as fun as it could be, which is a vital consideration in terms of team dynamics and system-wide adoption.

SUMMARY

- ▶ The critical enabler of a debrief-centric culture is Psychological Safety.

- ▶ High-Performing Teams require a focus on the truth.

- ▶ Accountability starts at the top, specifically with the leadership.

- ▶ A debrief-centric culture is enabled by a values system centered on Integrity.

- ▶ Everyone must buy in to the approach; the culture must embrace it.

CHAPTER 3

PROCESS REQUIREMENTS

DO WHAT YOU CAN WITH ALL YOU HAVE,
WHEREVER YOU ARE.

Theodore Roosevelt

Our fundamental principle is that a high-performing team is made up of people who are trusted and empowered to achieve the team's mission. Junior-level leaders are trusted and empowered to do what needs to be done to achieve success. The organization is less hierarchical, and power is distributed down to lower levels.

THE DEBRIEF FOCUSED APPROACH™

There is very little "Mother may I?" at play, and the expectation is that those on the front lines can and will make the right decisions. The military defines this arrangement as "Mission Command" and it begins with the top-level leadership outlining expectations in a very clear way—so that it becomes a shared mental model of what success looks like and how it can be quantified. Returning to *The Debrief-Focused Approach*™, we see that after the "Expectation of the Debrief", we're in the "Mission Planning" phase. This is critical; it is the process of planning, and not necessarily the resulting plan, that helps teams to anticipate the future and develop ways of dealing with any potential uncertainties.

The starting point for Planning in the context of Mission Command is the development of what we'll call "Commander's Intent." A clear understanding of Commander's Intent will allow the development of the actionable "Objectives" we'll set out to achieve. The facilitators of world-class Execution include Standards, Tactics and Checklists.

Definition of Success – Commander's Intent

Having a clear understanding of what success looks like empowers team members to each perform their part to achieve that future to the best of their ability. This future vision helps set the conditions for successfully navigating from Simple through Chaotic Domains. For reference, I've twice lived in Germany, and my first three years there were in the mid-1980's. The highways in Germany don't say "95N" or "25S," they say "Richtung Hamburg" or "Munich," where "Richtung" means direction. When driving on German highways prior to the GPS era, you really had to know *before you left* exactly where you were going, and where that location was in terms of the big picture, in order to get there, otherwise you were easily lost. How often do we find ourselves in a similar situation in our organizations? How often do we follow without an understanding of this envisioned future—and how often does that lead to wasted effort, resources and time, and ultimately cause extreme frustration? Commander's Intent provides this vision of where we're going and how to get there.

Chad Storlie, in his *Harvard Business Review* article on

Managing Uncertainty, shares this: "Commander's Intent describes how the Commander (read: CEO) envisions the battlefield at the conclusion of the mission. It shows what success looks like. Commander's Intent fully recognizes the chaos, lack of a complete information picture, changes in enemy situation, and other relevant factors that may make a plan either completely or partially obsolete when it is executed." Therefore, according to Storlie, "The role of Commander's Intent is to empower subordinates and guide their initiative and improvisation as they adapt the plan to the changed battlefield environment. Commander's Intent empowers initiative, improvisation, and adaptation by providing guidance of what a successful conclusion looks like. Commander's Intent is vital in chaotic, demanding, and dynamic environments." [52] So where does it come from? It comes from the top; the commander, the CEO.

Back in October of 2001, I had just landed from leading a combat mission over Iraq and was getting ready to debrief when I received a message to call my former commander at the Combined Air Operations Center (CAOC). I was exhausted after a long day of mission planning, not much sleep, the adrenaline rush of flying over hostile territory for 4+ hours on a 6.5-hour mission, and then leading the post-mission debrief. As soon as the debrief was complete, I called the number and my former commander let me know that he needed my help in the CAOC—immediately. Excited for a change of pace, I raced over to a massive facility I had never been in before. I had no idea I was about to work an additional 12 or so hours that night in support of our just-started operations in Afghanistan.

The CAOC is where we develop the Air Tasking Order—the document delivered to the Mission Commander that enables him or her to craft the execution plan for the following day. This is the plan that facilitates the continued progress towards the commander's End State. The progress is incremental; in other words, it may take months or even years to achieve the ultimate End State. And because of the complex nature of the battlefield, progress is achieved and measured in smaller chunks.

That facility was where we transformed strategy into the practical directions needed at the tactical level. Our commander, a three-star general, worked with his staff to develop his vision of the future and craft his Intent such that tactical experts like myself—who operated at the front-lines of the bat-tlespace—could then construct the tactical plans necessary to help him achieve his Ends. His staff worked hard to ensure that every mission we launched brought our collective team a step closer to the end goal, and that we achieved our goals as quickly as possible. The CAOC is where our commander worked to push forth his Intent along with the rest of the details we needed to plan and execute our daily missions. I was fortunate to have this real-time opportunity to witness battle planning in action, an opportunity that made an impression on me at an early stage in my professional development.

> **THE WORLD OF TOMORROW IS TOO COMPLEX TO BE SOLVED BY YESTERDAY'S ANSWER**

This approach follows Air Force Doctrine, which reads (among other things) that, "Operations are driven by desired ends (end states and objectives) and should be defined by the effects required to attain these ends, not just by what *available* forces or capabilities can do, nor by what the Air Force "customarily" does with a given set of forces." Additionally, "Commanders should realize they are dealing with interactively complex problems not solvable by deterministic or "checklist" approaches. Interactive complexity carries implications that are important for commanders to realize." [53] In other words, you must understand the effects that you're trying to achieve; don't limit yourself by trying to do things the way you've always done them. The world of tomorrow is too complex to be solved by yesterday's answer.

In business terms, consider the "End State" to be a company's "future position." The CEO's concern should be what this position is going to look like, and whether he and his company can achieve this desired future based on the current trajectory.[54] Michael E. Gerber, in his seminal work *The E-Myth Revisited*, addresses this point in his definition of the Strategic Objective. He calls it "the vision of the finished product that is and will be your business." He explains that, "It is a tool for measuring your progress toward a specific end...It is a template for your business, to make certain that the time you invest in it produces exactly what you want from it."[55] For further reading on Commander's Intent, I highly recommend the paper *Commander's Intent and Concept of Operations*, written by Majors Jonathan Chavous and Rich Dempsey, published in the November 2012-2013 *Military Review*.

The bottom line is that it always makes sense to start out

on a project, a mission, and every other aspect of life by knowing where you're going. This remains true regardless of how many technical aids you might have at your disposal. Most importantly, it really helps your team to know where you envision your organization going. This is the only way that they, armed with this important information, can then help either craft or perform the necessary tasks to help you get there.

How We Get There: Objectives

In the hierarchy of goals to tactics, the general outline looks like this, as outlined in columnist and book author Mikal Belicoves' piece in forbes.com[56]:

HEIRARCHY OF GOALS AND TACTICS
Mikal Belicoves', Forbes.com

Belicoves identifies Goals as "Broad, primary outcomes." Strategy is the "Approach you take to achieve a Goal." Objectives are "measurable steps you take to achieve a strategy" and Tactics are tools "you use in pursuing an Objective associated with a Strategy."[57] Given these definitions, we're well past the development of strategic goals and the crafting of strategy. We're describing the development of the tactical game plan, which is where our Objectives play such a critical role. Our Objectives, which must be both *achievable and measurable*, as well as *defined in time*, shape the way our tactics will be developed.

> ❝ OUR OBJECTIVES SERVED AS EXTREMELY CLEAR DEFINITIONS OF SUCCESS

I was on a typical mission back when I was a young Weapons Officer—the chief Instructor Pilot in the 27th Fighter Squadron, America's oldest continuously-serving fighter squadron. It was early in 2003, and our squadron was preparing to go to war in Iraq. My specific focus was on qualifying as many new 4-Ship Flight Leads as we could, so that we would have qualified leaders available to serve as Wingmen on our early combat missions. The intent was to grow extremely-qualified Wingmen, acknowledging that experience rules the day on a combat mission. Only our most experienced pilots would actually lead or serve as deputy leads in combat. Our approach was designed to rapidly accelerate individual growth, and collectively raise our squadron's capabilities.

Each one of these missions was a high-stress event—both because the men leading these missions understood what was at stake, and because we knew we had the urgency of time working against us. Since I was the senior Instructor Pilot, I flew on a lot of these missions as the "IP of record", the instructor responsible for determining whether or not the student passed the ride. As such, I was also responsible for debriefing the student on his performance, after *he* finished formally debriefing the team on *our* performance—from his perspective. I provided him *my* debrief of *his* mission planning, briefing, in-flight execution and debrief.

This is the standard qualification process in the fighter squadron. If you don't pass the ride, you get to do it again, and perhaps again, and maybe even again. At some point, we kick you out of the upgrade (and potentially out of the jet) if you don't have what it takes to succeed; there are only so many training missions we can allocate to a given individual before the squadron starts to suffer.

It was therefore an extremely exciting time for us in the 27th Fighter Squadron. Each of these mission briefings started the exact same way—we began with the Time-hack, the statement of the Mission, and a reading of our Objectives. It sounded something like this:

> *"3, 2, 1, Hack. Mission: 4-Ship Offensive Counter-Air. Objectives: 100% valid bombs on-target, on-time with no losses. 100% valid identification, Rules of Engagement adherence and weapons employment. 100% clear, correct and concise communications in accordance with governing directives."*

We started our mission briefings this way, every day, centering our collective focus on WHY we were there, and WHAT we needed to do to be successful. The briefed objectives were written on the board for use post-flight. *Everything* about the mission centered on our objectives. We reinforced our objectives so well that even now, many years removed from flying those missions, I can see the objectives as clear as they were back then. I still know exactly what we were aiming to achieve, and I can even recall what our typical challenges were in achieving mission success.

Our objectives served as extremely clear Definitions of Success. We defined success in plain terms, describing exactly what we needed to do en route to our End State, to make sure we achieved our Commander's Intent and successfully accomplished the mission.

Well-crafted Objectives describe both the *what* and the *how*. From what I've seen, most companies are really good at defining the what—"We need to achieve $XM in sales," or "We need to move XM tons of goods by such and such date," etc. What they don't define as well is the how. For instance, "We must sell $XM in Y amount of time, within our budget of $ZM, and we have to keep 99% of our team happy in the process." The foundation of this approach is centered on the fact that the WHAT, done in accordance with the HOW, should lead to *repeatable success*. It is also how we build our culture. In fact, the HOW is instrumental in building our culture.

From the flying example, the primary objective of achieving "100% valid bombs on-time, on-target with no losses" is supported by the follow-on objectives. It's one thing to drop all the bombs where they need to be dropped, within the appropriate drop window. But the real proof of expertise is making sure the bombs are dropped in accordance with all applicable laws (we refer to these as the "Rules of Engagement"), as well as within the appropriate drop parameters (necessary to ensure the bombs function properly). It so happens that there are defined parameters for employing or dropping bombs correctly, which means just dropping them isn't sufficient. The pilot has to drop them within the parameters to ensure they work as designed.

There is no doubt what the definition of success was on those particular missions. Now let's look at how things often transpire in the business world. We regularly have people in organizations—good organizations—who work feverishly on what they believe needs to be done in order to "do a good job." They often come in early and start working hard. They might not break from their work for hours; sometimes they miss lunch and eating snack bars to get by, all the while working hard. They might leave past normal business hours, continuing to work to accomplish what they believe needs to be accomplished. When asked why what they're doing matters, they can provide a good explanation, one which satisfies the team...and onward we press. All too often, though, those great sounding explanations are misguided, fed by unclear expectations of what *actually* needs to be accomplished.

Unfortunately, these good people who are working so hard on their incredibly important work are often not supporting their company's real objectives. According to a 2016 world-wide Gallup poll "only about half of employees strongly agree that they know what is expected of them at work."[58] If this is indeed the case, think of all the wasted work; all the employees who burn out because management allows them to slave away on projects that don't support the objectives. Amy Gallo, contributing editor at Harvard Business Review notes, "Employees want to see how their work contributes to larger corporate objectives," and this is impossible if we don't start with these objectives in mind.[59]

Stephen Covey speaks of this same basic concern in his worldwide bestseller, *The 7 Habits of Highly Effective People*. The second habit he proposes is to "Begin with the End in Mind." Covey says it perfectly when he defines this as, "…start[ing] with a clear understanding of your destination." He explains that, "It's incredibly easy to get caught up in an activity trap, in the busyness of life, to work harder and harder at climbing the ladder of success only to discover it's leaning against the wrong wall. It is possible to be busy—very busy—without being very effective."[60] If we're honest with ourselves, we've all seen it, and we've all probably practiced it and unwittingly promoted this senseless "doing" without a purpose. Setting clear, achievable and measurable objectives helps us get on the right track and do meaningful work that moves us and our organizations forward.

Those immersed in the world of complexity theory argue that it's impossible to know what the future will look like, and therefore impossible to set objectives. I can see where this might be the case at a strategic level, but I strongly disagree with the argument on an operational or tactical one. In fact, this point reinforces the need to debrief continuously, allowing for a constant review of whether or not we're making any progress. Once we understand the strategy and have an End State to attain, even if it's fuzzy and unclear, we can absolutely chart our progress towards that End State by defining clear, achievable, and measurable objectives. It's just a question of finding the correct objectives that help move towards the potentially "fuzzy" End State.

Others I've spoken with are opposed to setting objectives because there's a line of thought that says, "once the objective is achieved, the team will stop working." I would argue that in some circumstances, stopping once the objective is achieved is entirely appropriate. I've taught my F-15 students to not stick around in "Bad Guy Land" any longer than necessary, and I've debriefed people for remaining in harm's way once the objective was achieved. In this case it is absolutely appropriate to quit (return to base, in fighter terms) as soon as the objective is achieved.

I also understand that given the way certain organizations are structured—think sales organizations—it's entirely plausible that team members will be satisfied with having achieved an objective, leading to ending a sales process early. I can see them shifting their efforts towards lining up business that they can count towards the next tracking period. Even if this approach doesn't benefit the organization as a whole, it is a sound strategy for the individual, given the associated compensation and incentive structure. This, then, needs to be brought into focus at the leadership level—is this type of compensation and incentive structure the right one for the organization at the strategic level? Does it promote accelerated performance, innovation and true growth? These are good questions for leaders to consider when adopting an objectives-based methodology and operating system.

I would personally argue that in non-combat situations, there is great benefit to incentivizing people to keep pushing, to embrace exceeding the current objective as the obvious next objective. People with this approach don't stop working because continuing on means setting a higher bar, demonstrating even greater levels of success. I maintain that the values at the front of this book inform this line of thought; my fundamental assumption is that people are striving for excellence in all they do, and always work with Integrity. I have never been a part of a team that had time left on the clock and didn't keep looking to put points on the board—to set a new limit, a new boundary. Can you imagine an Olympic athlete slowing down once they were 1 second faster than the fastest time? Winners don't stop…the goal is to be the best you can be. Period.

How We Get There: Standards & Tactics

Along the road to winning, we can make use of Standards, Tactics and Checklists to guide our approaches and streamline our efforts. Standards are a way of codifying how "our tribe" does its business. I appreciate the "tribe" analogy because it describes how a squadron identifies itself and operates. Every tribe has its own unique view of the world, its own understanding of what's important and why...a view that helps define who the tribe is, and how it intends to operate in its environment. Fighter squadrons codify a portion of this understanding as their Standards. Standards help us to create consistency and repeatability in what we do, so we don't have to design everything from scratch every time we do it. Adherence to these standards helps to train new members of the tribe on how "we" do businesses. Every single U.S. fighter squadron has a list of administrative and tactical standards which describe how each squadron chooses to do the various things they must complete on every mission. Where variances can occur, they will. Whether it's the spacing the pilots will use while taxiing to and from the runway, to the radio frequency every wingman is expected to be on during different phases of flight, to the formation the pilots will fly coming back home ...the way each tribe does these things is codified and considered to be "standard."

Tactics are methods that are proven to work, those we know will allow us to succeed in accomplishing our mission. Tactics are agreed upon by all of the tribes gathered together as a unified whole. They therefore remain the same amongst all of the tribes and allow for uniformity in performance whenever tribes exchange members (which we often do in the fighter world). Tactics are codified in manuals and studied by all practitioners, from seasoned warriors to new additions to the team. They are modified and updated based on changes in either the threats' or the tribes' capabilities, as well as any advances in approaches. Fighter tactics specifically outline the options available to the pilot that we know will work, based on the threat or threats that we're facing. Where Standards apply universally, tactics are chosen and utilized based on need. In all cases, tactics are a proven means of employment. They are vetted and approved by leaders and form the core of how our successful fighter force operates. Together, these documents define how our tribe is going to dominate in any domain anywhere on the planet.

Tactics are not at all unique to fighter organizations. One company I worked with uses tactics set forth as their "core sales approach". New salespeople are taught this approach, one that has been developed and tested over decades of study, to help them achieve their desired outcomes. Another company I've been associated with has a similarly focused approach they teach all of their salespeople—an approach that is based on the science of sales, proven over time to be effective. The value of each of these sets of tactics is that they're proven to work. And while there may be room for adaptation and variance, sticking to the fundamentals is usually the best avenue to success. Tactics enable success.

What's key is that everyone in the organization must be extremely familiar with both the applicable squadron Standards and the overall employment Tactics. This familiarization process takes time, training, study, and practice. As previously noted, standards and tactics are not static—they evolve constantly, based on updated equipment, software, threat capabilities, etc., which means that the tribe has to evolve as well. This in-turn ensures that the team is always learning and that nobody stays static. While it can be challenging at times, it's vital in the greater context.

I will also emphasize this point: having standards doesn't mean "blind" compliance or rote actions. Standards are a starting point, and tactics are the menu of proven options that we know get the job done. In the complex world of fighter aviation, they provide us the springboard from which we launch to dominate. But Flight Leads are absolutely permitted to choose to brief approaches that differ from the Standards. Team members may think up new Tactics. Both are subject to approval before being implemented, but the process is certainly not static and always remains open to improvement.

Where Did These Concepts Come From?

To answer this question on the fighter pilot side, we should return to World War I. During this war, both sides fielded a brand-new weapon—the airplane. Because of its recency (the Wright brothers first flew in 1903) pilots had to learn as they went how to both stay alive and defeat the enemy without pushing the airplane beyond its relatively frail limits. Reading Capt. Eddie Rickenbacker's *Fighting the Flying Circus*, tells the story of the American experience in France, which makes it clear that every day was an opportunity to learn. It's also clear that each day many of the more seasoned pilots shared their hard-fought lessons learned with newer pilots. I believe it's safe to say that with every day the pilots of the very first fighter squadrons refined their processes until some became procedures. These procedures eventually became standards and tactics, each of which formed the foundation from which U.S. pilots eventually ruled the skies. Since 1953, no U.S. serviceperson has been attacked from the air. We've built on those early standards and tactics with every passing mission, month and year. It's now ingrained but traces its roots back to the early 20th Century.

Where do these ideas come from in business? And why does any of this matter outside of fighter aviation? Simply put: Because systemization and standardization are critical for businesses to function properly. It's what Michael Gerber emphasized throughout his *E-Myth* series, referring to this process as a company's Management System or "how we do it here", which is also "the core competency your company must possess."[61] The basis for Gerber's approach is the McDonald's franchise, which he recommends as the model for all companies to follow. Not that all companies need to make hamburgers, far from it. Gerber's point is that all companies should have their own specific, defined way of doing what they do. This way is codified and followed to the letter, ensuring that everyone who ever comes in contact with the company, anywhere on the planet, gets the same exceptional service—something to be excited about. Just like McDonald's. In fact, the whole Root Cause of McDonalds' success over decades has been its ability to provide the exact same food at any of its restaurants almost anywhere on the planet. You generally know what you're getting at McDonald's, and it's something that people like…and, if you're my 4-year-old, you also get really excited about it.

Checklists

In addition to Standards and Tactics, we in the flying world depend on checklists to be safe. There's a really good reason for this that physician and author Atul Gawande does a fantastic job highlighting it in his bestselling work, *The Checklist Manifesto*. Gawande outlines the tale of the procurement of the B-17 bomber back in 1935. The short story is that airplane cockpits and flight procedures can be complicated, and the B-17 was extremely complicated for its time. This came back to haunt the B-17 program at a critical point in its development. The day the test version of the B-17 was to demonstrate its effectiveness over the other bomber candidates (it was the hands-down favorite to win the Army's new bomber fly-off competition), it "roared down the tarmac, lifted off smoothly, and climbed sharply to three hundred feet. Then it stalled, turned on one wing, and crashed in a fiery explosion. Two of the five crew members died, including the pilot, Major Ployer P. Hill." It's important to note that the airplane was in outstanding shape and there was no mechanical failure. The issue was that Major Hill had overlooked a critical step in the start-up sequence: he had forgotten to release a locking mechanism that affected the elevator and rudder controls. As a result of this tragedy, Boeing lost the flight competition and nearly went bankrupt. The eventual fix was pretty ingenious: a group of test pilots came up with a pilot checklist, step-by-step checks for all critical phases of flight. The US Army eventually purchased almost 13,000 of these airplanes, a program saved by the development of the checklist.[62]

If pilots don't follow procedures, there's a good chance we put ourselves and our crews in really dangerous positions. On one particular mission, I was shocked when I discovered that I had not turned on the pitot heat—a necessary procedure to ensure our critical flight instruments work regardless of external environmental factors. On another day, I realized upon landing that I had not been buckled into my ejection seat— which would have led to my death if I had pulled the ejection handles. Why did I make these critical mistakes? Most likely because I was distracted by something and simply forgot to complete my procedure. It's not that I was intentionally negligent, nor ignoring procedures. The fact is that I am a human being and, as such, am immensely fallible. I make mistakes; we all do. Checklists are designed to help combat this fallibility and, when used properly, do a magnificent job of keeping us fallible humans on task.

There's a lot going on in the heat of an emergency, and the airplane is always moving forward. As pilots, we're trained to handle these situations without getting rushed into a position where we make irreversible mistakes. In fact, the first step of any emergency is generally to try to slow things down a bit, both literally and figuratively. The concept is to do the right thing at the right time—to critically analyze the situation before deciding which appropriate action to take. Then, we pull out our checklists to ensure we do everything required in the proper sequence.

Part of the purpose of checklists is to ensure we don't miss critical steps during time-critical and high-stress situations.

Some checklists are so important we commit them to memory. In certain sectors of the flying world these are called BOLD-FACE or CAPS procedures. These procedures are the most mission-critical items that must be done correctly the first time to maximize the chance of successfully handling a problem in the time available.

Checklists in Business

The world we're living in and dealing with is too complex to handle without checklists in the business world. Certain organizations—hospital staff, emergency responders, aircrew, etc.—require them more than others. But whatever your industry, checklists can be tremendously useful in a variety of settings. For example, one company I'm working with sells seminars and workshops across the country. They handle everything tied to the process, from the initial outreach and marketing, to the booking of hotel rooms, to the facilitation of the workshops and the post-workshop follow up. Their work requires them to sell and host multiple workshops, sometimes on consecutive weeks and in geographically-diverse locations.

Achieving client fulfillment is too complicated for the company to operate without checklists. Missing a step along the way may very likely mean that a client's experience will be less than perfect. Upset clients tend to leave bad reviews, and in a competitive setting those reviews can mean less business. The cycle can be vicious. This company desperately needs checklists to ensure every client has an excellent experience from the moment they first hear the offer, to the point at which they receive their hand-written follow-up card and associated offer for follow-on services.

I worked with a mortgage company that used checklists to ensure the building was secured appropriately at the end of the day. The checklist was designed to be filled out by whoever closed the building down for the night. There was a space for that person's initials and closing time, along with space to check off that individual closing items—clients' folders being properly filed, cabinets being locked, and lights being turned off—were accomplished. While this is an exceptionally basic example, having this system in place helped ensure both the security of clients' personal information as well as compliance with State and Federal law. The best part is that implementing this kind of process costs nothing.

From the shut-down and lock-up procedures at the end of the work day, to the way in which retail workers stock shelves and check inventory, to the set-up and hosting of an elaborate event—the applications are limitless, and truly apply everywhere. Checklists ensure uniformity and standards' adherence. Some argue that they hamper individualism; I maintain that they're literally life-savers across-the-board.

"Teamwork," not "Taskwork"

Another important distinction for us to understand is that there's a difference between "Teamwork" and "Taskwork". For this, I'll turn to the work being done in academia on *The Science of Teamwork* for a few critical definitions. To begin with, let's look at some definitions of what a Team is. According to one group of researchers, "Teams are 'a distinguishable set of two or more people who interact, dynamically, interdependently, and adaptively toward a common and valued goal/objective/mission.'[63] Katzenbach and Smith, authors of the seminal work, *The Wisdom of Teams*, offer a similar definition: "A team is a small group of people (typically fewer than twenty) with complimentary skills committed to a common purpose and set of specific performance goals. Its members are committed to working with each other to achieve the team's purpose and hold each other fully and jointly accountable for the team's results." [64] Both of these definitions capture the primary components of teams—"multiple individuals, interdependencies, and a shared goal..." [65]

> MOST TEAMS ARE **"** FOCUSED ON TASKWORK AND NOT ON THE TEAMWORK FUNDAMENTALS THAT ALLOW TEAMS TO THRIVE

Next, it's critical to understand that effective teams

perform both taskwork and teamwork, where Taskwork is defined as "the performance of specific tasks that team members need to complete in order to achieve team goals. In particular, tasks represent the world-related activities that individuals or teams engage in as an essential function of their organizational role."[66] Examples of tasks might be the creation of a marketing plan that supports the grand sales effort, or the completion of the operations manual that helps the team understand the operations process. Groups of people might have been involved in the development of both, but the fact that tasks that were physically performed is not necessarily evidence that teamwork took place.

Finally, Teamwork "focuses more on the shared behaviors (i.e., what team members *do*), attitudes (i.e., what team members *feel or believe*), and cognitions (i.e., what team members *think or know*) that are necessary for teams to accomplish these tasks."[67] My observation is that most teams are focused on Taskwork and not on the Teamwork fundamentals that allow teams to thrive.

One of the many take-aways from *The Science of Teamwork* is that there are specific things teams need to know and physically do in order to be effective. As authors Dr. Eduardo Salas, Denise Reyes and Susan McDaniel note, "Even if a team is made up of experts, it can still fail if they do not know how to cooperate, coordinate and communicate well together. To ensure the improvement and maintenance of effective team functioning, the organization must implement team development interventions and evaluate relevant team outcomes with robust diagnostic measurement."[68] As previously discussed, the debrief is a mechanism that provides these development-interventions and allows us to focus on both Teamwork and Taskwork. Its power is not limited to a focus on desired outcomes but also in building and maintaining effective teams.

CONCLUSION

Where the previous chapter outlined the cultural and value requirements for a debrief to thrive, this chapter provided the necessary process foundations. In short, successful organizations that want to practice Accountable Leadership should use Standards, Tactics and Checklists, as well as understand the difference between Teamwork and Taskwork. They should truly focus on developing Teamwork. This concludes Part I, and now we'll move into the details of *HOW* to accomplish a successful Debrief.

SUMMARY

▶ The definition of success is called Commander's Intent

▶ Objectives help chart the path towards achieving success

▶ Standards and Tactics help us along the way

▶ Checklists help ensure humans do the right thing in time-critical and challenging circumstances

▶ There's a difference between Taskwork and Teamwork. Most organizations focus only on Taskwork and don't truly understand Teamwork.

PART TWO
THE ART OF
THE DEBRIEF

CHAPTER 4

A MORE IN-DEPTH LOOK AT A FIGHTER PILOT DEBRIEF

"

INSANITY: DOING THE SAME THING OVER AND OVER AGAIN AND EXPECTING DIFFERENT RESULTS.

Unknown

Flying high-performance fighter aircraft is both a physical and mental challenge. In terms of the physical, fighter aircraft are engineered to push the human body beyond its natural limits. After a fighter mission, specifically after a "dogfighting" mission, we come back drenched in sweat, dehydrated, our limbs full of capillaries that popped during the high-G loading portions of the mission, leaving red marks we affectionately call "G-easles". Depending on the mission, the neck and back can become extremely sore. I don't know of a single fighter pilot who, after a career flying aircraft capable of rapidly exerting and then sustaining up to nine times the force of gravity on the human body, doesn't have at least moderate neck and back problems. I once flew in an F-16, piloted by a senior instructor from an allied country who had zero feeling in his left arm or hand. None whatsoever. He told me I could stab his arm and he would feel nothing.

On the mental side, one of the many challenges facing the fighter pilot is being able to quickly assess—while under extreme "G" forces, and while maneuvering in three dimensions—whether an adversary is in a position to employ weapons against him. Making this *critical* assessment upside down and looking backwards over your shoulder, while simultaneously making radio calls to your formation mate and checking on your altitude to make sure you're not going to hit the ground, can be extremely taxing—and knowing that *everything* depends on making this assessment correctly can be especially so. Then there's the need to keep track of everyone on your team across the entire airspace, which is one of the main challenges that Mission Commanders face. Interestingly, while the mental side of the job is often overlooked, it also happens to be the single most *important* part of the job. The people who succeed at flying in this domain can reach out of their individual cockpits and command a battlespace. Those who can't figure out how to do this quickly find themselves flying something else or, in the best case, not advancing very far in their qualifications.

I share this not to complain or to brag, even though it might sound like a bit of both. This insight should help to paint the picture that at the end of one of these missions the body has been physically and mentally *punished*. And at the point where one would otherwise decide to relax and call it a day, we then begin the real work of the mission. I'm neither being dramatic, nor am I trying to make more of this than I should—the real learning begins once the mission is over. Everything that happened in the sky created the truths or the facts that we'll now spend our time dissecting, reviewing through various lenses, all in a disciplined effort to figure out where we didn't do as well as we could have. The facts we create while airborne leads to the analysis we do in the debrief room. And this analysis is the gold that leads to continuous improvement, the continuation of our tribe, a culture centered on truth, and all of the good things that enable our collective success!

An Introduction to the Formal Debrief Process

I'll now introduce you to the basic approach used in a fighter pilot debrief. This brief example will walk you through the beginning phase of a "dogfight" debrief—the "one vs. one" profile I first mentioned in the "Pre-brief" chapter, where two pilots try to maneuver against each other—the goal being that one pilot employs simulated weapons against the other. The overall flight may last just shy of an hour, but the tactical maneuvering, and specifically each individual "dogfight" (there can sometimes be 5 or 6 of these fights on a given mission) typically lasts only a few minutes.

On this particular mission, one fighter who we'll call the "Offensive Fighter," starts approximately 3,000 feet behind and to the right of the other, "Defensive Fighter." One point of this exercise is to teach the Defensive Fighter how to survive when starting from an *extremely* defensive situation—something that is not only very possible, but one in which the best pilots can even switch and become the Offensive Fighter. The other point is to teach the Offensive Fighter how to finish the job and transition from an extremely offensive position into one where he appropriately employs weapons to "win" the fight.

We'll look at this in the context of an instructor-student scenario, but the same principles hold true on any mission profile we fly. When it comes to the objectives for this type of mission, the objectives are geared towards the defensive side of things if the student is the Defensive Fighter; if the student is the Offensive Fighter, the objectives are set accordingly. The important item to note is that the emphasis is on the student, and his or her ability to achieve the objectives. In the following section there will be terms I don't define because they're not critical for our understanding of the process. I would ask simply that you review the overall flow of the debrief, looking at the integrity demonstrated by the Flight Lead as well as the process of both capturing the truth and then utilizing that truth for mutual benefit.

In this case we'll say our student is the Defensive Fighter, and in the mission briefing, I, as the Instructor Pilot or IP, would have briefed objectives that were very similar to the following:

TACTICAL OBJECTIVES:

* DEFEAT THE INITIAL ATTACK

* DENY SUBSEQUENT OPPORTUNITIES FOR THE OFFENSIVE FIGHTER TO ATTACK

* ESCAPE FROM THE FIGHT, NEUTRALIZE THE FIGHT OR BECOME THE OFFENSIVE FIGHTER

"Tape Review"

We'll begin our review at the point where we've landed and finished our Maintenance Debriefs. Following maintenance debrief, we would then make our way into what we called "tape review." This is where we look at digital playback of our engagements—the capture of critical data displayed on our Head's-Up Displays, RADAR, and other systems that help us find, track, target, and destroy the enemy while keeping us safe. During tape review we set short timelines that force us to gather our data as quickly as possible. The idea is to debrief as efficiently as possible and learn our lessons, which then feed into the mission planning for our next mission.

The point of tape review is to gather our individual

versions of the "facts" of the mission. I say "our individual versions" because where there is more than one airplane flying, there is more than one version of the facts. This is the case in any human endeavor—we each have our own individual perspective and understanding of what is taking place around us. The main point of tape review is to gather the relevant data associated with our particular understanding of what happened, so that we can combine this with the other perspective(s) and *arrive at the truth of what actually occurred* in-flight.

Functionally, we review our tapes while transcribing the critical data we captured during playback onto paper. This transcription involves depicting where our airplanes were in relation to key points and other airplanes throughout the fight. In addition, we document any critical information such as weapons launches or releases, defensive responses/maneuvers, and anything else deemed critical such as near-misses, violations of safety rules, and any other safety concerns.

The purpose of tape review is to arm ourselves with everything necessary to have an effective debrief. Tape review takes time, and time is always in short supply—but of all the things we did on a mission, this was always one of the most valuable because the truth begins to take shape during this process. We are often surprised at the disparity between what we "remembered" happening on the mission, and what the tapes demonstrated to be the case. This tends to be just as valid in all areas of life—we think things happened a certain way, but when we review the data, it turns out our recollection isn't always right. As such, we might spend 45 minutes reviewing our tapes for a mission that had maybe 30 minutes' worth of tactical events.

Following tape review, we meet in the debrief room, where the Flight Lead is clearly prepared to lead the debrief. This means that he or she has completed an effective tape review but has also considered many additional factors. These might include issues with planning, the pre-mission briefing and those parts of the mission we don't spend time reviewing in tape review, namely the "going and coming" to and from the airspace, and any other "administrative" points that went beyond the pure tactical mission. In short, the leader takes time during his or her tape review to actively self-reflect and critically assess both personal and team performance. The point of this is to be able to share it in the team debrief.

Why This Matters in Business

The first client I ever introduced this "Tape Review" process to confessed to me that before he went into the kinds of meetings he viewed as debriefs, he typically didn't prepare at all. He was accustomed to simply showing up and hoping for the best, confident in his ability to accurately recall all of the relevant data. He had achieved great personal and organizational success while operating in this manner, and his company was (and still is) performing magnificently. All that said, he immediately saw the value of the "Tape Review" process. From what I could tell he realized that this as something that could help improve his performance and achieve even higher highs. He became an early adopter of this process, as were several members of his leadership team, specifically because the science behind this process makes sense.

The danger of going into a debrief unarmed with the best available version of the facts of what happened is that the human brain, and the memories it forms, is highly vulnerable to error. According to Joyce Lacey and Craig Stark in their article, "The Neuroscience of Memory: Implications for the Courtroom," memory is a reconstructive process that is susceptible to distortion.[69] In their research they refer to a study conducted by H. Ebbinghaus, whose work demonstrated "that people are unable to retrieve roughly 50% of information one hour after encoding." In addition, there's a host of information that demonstrates that the information that is retrieved is often distorted. Among the multitude of fascinating revelations about memory and the human inability to properly recollect is the fact that we tend to filter what we perceive based on our existing knowledge and experience, leading to a biased recollection of the facts.[70] In short, we can't access everything we need, and what we do need to access can be warped by our internal biases, as well as by the passage of time and advancing age. The authors cite numerous examples, among which was the inability of military professionals to correctly identify their interrogators after being released from a mock prisoner of war camp. Despite having a clear view of the individual over the course of a 30 to 40-minute interrogation, "only approximately a third of the identifications were correct." In addition, these individuals were highly-susceptible to misinformation, a factor that "increased the likelihood of a false identification."[71] Has this ever happened to you, either personally or professionally? Can you recall a situation where you and someone else involved in an event recalled it differently? My guess is that you have, because this happens to all of us. Our challenge is to understand the implications, specifically when discussing debriefs.

Armed with this information, we now consider the implications of running an accountability process with only our memory to rely on. Chances are we're going to not only miss a lot of critical information, but we're also going to share inaccurate information. Using a "Tape Review" process to help prepare will go a long way towards enabling an efficient, correct and rewarding debrief. We'll discuss some techniques as we go through the process.

A Sample Dialogue Incorporating Coaching

Let's return to our "dogfighting" example. Once both pilots have completed their respective "Tape Reviews", the Instructor Pilot (IP) closes the door and begins **a dialogue** with his Wingman (WG) that might look like this:

IP: *Welcome back. Today's debrief flow will be standard—we'll cover the Brief, admin both to and from the training area, admin in the training area, any Training Rule violations, and then we'll debrief the tactical portion of our mission with a focus on your ability to achieve today's objectives. If that makes sense, let's go back to the brief...do you have any questions or comments on anything I briefed this morning?*

WG: *No.*

IP: *OK, well, I've got two points for myself. First of all, the briefing went three minutes too long. That's outside of our standards which, as you know, say the briefing should be 65 +/- two minutes. I exceeded that. Why does this matter? Because every minute that I brief over is a minute you don't have to, say, go to the bathroom or grab a drink on the way to the jet or do a thorough pre-flight. Why did I brief too long? Frankly, it's because I didn't practice enough. I briefed long on the first part of my briefing, and didn't adjust by either speeding up the second half or cutting out some less-important information. My fix for this is to practice my briefing several times before the next mission, as well as to add timing marks to my briefing guide. I'll hold myself to those timing marks to ensure I meet the overall timing objective. Does this make sense?*

WG: *Absolutely.*

IP: *Good. Second, when I briefed you that I would let you lead our formation back to practice at least one instrument approach and landing, I failed to address the fuel implications of doing so. I never adjusted our fuels to provide enough for a practice approach, which is why we came home having skipped this part of the mission. With your check ride coming up I failed to maximize your training because of my poor pre-mission planning, and I apologize. I didn't look at this week's schedule until a few minutes prior to the brief. I saw the check ride, and*

I made a mental note to add an instrument approach to our profile—I just didn't take the necessary steps to facilitate it. In short, I didn't plan for the additional fuel required to perform this approach. Next time I will bring upcoming check rides and grade book reviews into my cross-check during mission planning so that I can adjust our fuel calculations accordingly. I'll be happy to talk to your flight commander and mention that I failed to help you prepare...I can see if we can move your check ride back if you'd like.

WG: *It's no problem, really. I'm scheduled for an instrument simulator mission later this afternoon, and I'm flying another ride tomorrow where I can easily get a few approaches in at the end. I'll be fine, though I appreciate your words.*

IP: *Gotcha. OK—just know that I recognize the error and will make corrections. That's all I have for the mission briefing, unless you can think of anything else.*

WG: *Nothing else from my perspective.*

IP: *All right, then. In terms of our ground admin, I missed you on the very first check-in on ground frequency. Can you tell me what happened there?*

WG: *Yes. I was talking with my crew chief and didn't realize it was time to taxi until after I missed the check-in call.*

IP: *All right. As you know, our squadron standards state that we should be ready on ground frequency at check-in time unless we're working a problem, in which case* *we need to advise our flight lead what's happening. Just to be clear—were you working on a problem?*

WG: *No, not at all. I got caught up in chatting about my crew chief's next assignment—he just found out he's moving to Alaska in a few months and is really excited. I just flat out missed the call.*

IP: *Totally understood. All I can offer you is that even though you want to maintain a good rapport with your crew chief, we also need to represent our squadron appropriately. Everyone hears us on Ground control frequency. When a formation member misses a check-in, we look like we don't have our act together. Most importantly, however, it shows that we're not tight as a formation. My personal technique is to try to be disconnected from the intercom at two to three minutes prior to check-in. I would say that going forward you need to work on being aware of your timing, prioritizing where you're focusing your attention based on where we are on the mission timeline. Lead-turn it and make sure you and your crew chief are on the same page. Pre-brief him on when he can expect you to sign off and transition to mission-focus. Make sense?*

WG: *Absolutely. I knew I was pushing it, but I lost track and allowed our chatting to take priority. I won't make that mistake again.*

IP: *OK, good. Otherwise our taxi out to the runway was uneventful. Takeoff looked good and good job on your rejoin—it was smooth and efficient. Your subsequent* radio check-ins on the way to the airspace were timely and crisp. I have nothing for the takeoff, rejoin, and departure or anything else on into the airspace...it was all uneventful. Do you have anything for me going out to the airspace?

WG: One question. In the brief I was pretty sure you told me to rejoin to your right side but when I did you immediately told me to take a position on the left. Did I mess that up?

IP: Good question. And no, you didn't mess anything up—based on our updated clearance I knew we would be making a non-standard turn to the right on departure and I had you take position on the left to make it more comfortable to you. As you start thinking about becoming a flight lead yourself, consider the implications of updated clearances on how you're going to organize your formation. Make sense?

WG: Makes perfect sense. I agree that I need to start thinking like a flight lead in preparation for my upgrade in the near-future.

IP: Cool. All right, in terms of us coming home then, our initial rejoin and exit from the airspace was fine. Everything was solid until we began our descent back towards the field. Let's spend a couple of minutes talking about that close pass with that formation of A-10s. The first I knew of those guys was when you called them out to me, about 500-1000 feet before I descended directly into their flight path. Tell me what you saw.

WG: *Well, I was looking at you, trying to maintain my formation spacing, while scanning around your aircraft. About the time we rolled out after the left-hand turn my peripheral vision caught some movement from below and behind you. When I focused there, I saw the other formation that we were on the collision course with and immediately made the radio call to you to level-off.*

IP: *Outstanding. Your combination of visual lookout and directive radio call to me is the reason why I'm here leading this debrief and not at the hospital after my mid-air with an A-10! There is no doubt in my mind that I would have descended straight into his flight path and we would have hit. So you know, I contacted the flight lead from the other formation and he had no idea whatsoever that we were there. As you know, the A-10 has no RADAR, and he was busy looking over his shoulder, checking the status of his formation. He never saw our formation until after approach control gave him a 30-degree check turn to the left. I'll reiterate: your call was the ONLY reason why I didn't descend directly on top of him. I've filed a Hazardous Air Traffic Report with the Safety Office and I'm going to submit you for a safety award for your work today! That was world-class, and you can rest well tonight knowing that you are the reason disaster was averted! Any questions or additional comments?*

WG: *No, no questions. I appreciate the feedback and certainly appreciate the safety award submission.*

IP: *Brother, it's the least I can do...and I'd also like you to brief this scenario on Friday during our pilot meeting. You deserve to share this story of success, and we all need to reinforce the fact that visual lookout is absolutely vital during ALL phases of flight, not just during tactical maneuvering. Not only are you today's hero, but you're also going to help us all stay sharp by sharing this story.*

WG: *Thank you very much.*

IP: *Otherwise, once we were clear of the A-10s, I thought landing and taxi back to parking were both uneventful. I have nothing else to add on our recovery, do you?*

WG: *Nothing else.*

IP: *OK, good. In terms of airspace admin, I think we were mostly clean except for the setup of our second engagement. It took you a long time to get into position on this one, and we wasted a lot of gas. What happened?*

WG: *I lost sight of you after you called 'Knock-it-off' and took a while figuring out where you were.*

IP: *All right, you lost sight. Did you call out that you lost me?*

WG: *No, I didn't.*

IP: *Why not?*

WG: *I figured if I just gave it a minute I'd find you. I didn't think we were in a dangerous situation, and I felt confident that with just a little patience I would find you. As it was, I didn't see you again until I climbed all the way up to our starting altitude.*

IP: *OK. This is something we need to fix. You absolutely cannot afford to be flying around without seeing me. Imagine that I had also lost sight of you and kept that information to myself. Or consider the implication of me losing radio contact with you. Now there would be two of us flying around, neither seeing the other one in a relatively small piece of airspace. The chances of us hitting would be huge. The first step you need to take when you lose sight is to call it out. There is no harm or foul here. I'll do my very best to talk your eyes onto me. If you call it out and you hear nothing from me, your next best option while repeating your call is to remain at your last altitude and to use your on-board systems to figure out how far away we are from one another. You're looking for our distance to increase as I climb, as opposed to closing. Does this make sense?*

WG: *It absolutely makes a ton of sense...I know this, but I was so confident I'd see you any second that I sort of lost track of time. We're lucky you kept sight of me throughout.*

IP: *OK. I'm glad it all worked out and that we've talked about this here. Fortunately, it didn't cost us, and you know what to focus on for next time. That's all I have for airspace admin. In terms of Training Rule violations I don't have anything that came out of my tape review.*

> *Unless you saw something in your tapes, we'll continue to evaluate those items as we go through the rest of the debrief. Please let me know if you see a violation I don't catch as we go back through the tapes on each engagement.*

WG: *Will-do!*

IP: *All right, that closes out our admin. Let's now turn to the core of our mission today, and we'll start with a reminder of our tactical objectives. As I briefed you this morning, your objectives as the Defensive Fighter on today's mission were to:*

> > *Defeat the Initial Attack*
>
> > *Deny Subsequent Opportunities for the Offensive Fighter to Attack*
>
> > *To Escape from the fight, Neutralize the fight or Become the Offensive Fighter*

> *We'll be evaluating your ability to achieve one, two or all of these objectives as we go through each of the engagements. Now, let's begin our reconstruction of the first engagement...*

From this point onward, the debrief gets more detailed. Because the tactical details of a dogfighting mission are well-beyond the scope of what we need to learn, I'll stop and emphasize a few key points from this part of the debrief:

▶ The IP is self-aware, up-front and honest regarding his own faults, making the entire debrief process a non-threatening event by creating real-time psychological safety;

▶ The IP "debriefs to Standards" during the administrative portion of the debrief—there are no stated objectives here, other than to do things according to all established Standards, regulations and operating manuals. This is why it's critical to have these codified;

▶ The IP doesn't just identify issues, he proposes solutions, coaching his Wingman to success;

▶ The IP is quick to praise, taking extra steps to recognize superior performance. This is not an artificial process, however, and there is no effort to try to "sandwich" a negative comment between two good comments—it's all just honest assessments of the team's efforts;

▶ The IP does more in his tape review time than the wingman, reviewing and analyzing everything from mission planning through execution;

▶ The IP is in charge and is clearly the leader. That said, the Wingman is just as important to this process. The Wingman performed a function and has an important perspective of what took place. Today's Wingman is tomorrow's Flight Lead and next week's Instructor. The

Wingman's knowledge is key, and his development is critical. The Wingman speaks when given the opportunity and is an essential part of the discussion.

In terms of timing, the dialogue I've outlined here probably lasted about five minutes. This is usually the easiest part of the debrief, and the one that actually counts the *least* in the "big-picture" of the mission, because these are the items that precede tactical execution. On a fighter mission, the start, taxi, takeoff, departure, and then the reverse are all part of basic airmanship. *It's expected* that all of this goes well and there usually won't be much to talk about. It's not the point of our training, but we still take time to review how we did because there are always things we can improve on, and occasionally even critical areas to highlight like a near-miss. Because it's not our focus, we don't spend as much time on it. Time is always of the essence and we need to spend it wisely. It's the next part of the debrief that really gets our attention—so that's where we'll focus our efforts.

How This Applies in Business

We're all looking to improve performance in business; however, our leaders frequently struggle with how to inspire their teams to make necessary changes. One of the problems we face is that we don't often know how to pass along constructive criticism without losing our teammates' trust and upsetting the people we rely on. This fear leads us to tend to shy away from these conversations. And while this tendency is understandable, it's not doing anyone any favors.

The great news is that the debrief process both institutionalizes and "regularizes" the process that helps us have these challenging conversations. In addition, it provides a mechanism for open and honest exchanges that make our teams stronger, because leaders feel safe to share their failures while the rest of the team feels the necessary psychological safety to admit their errors.

Let's return to one of the companies I've mentioned earlier, the one where the leaders share personal and professional challenges at the beginning of their meetings. What's really striking to me about this firm is that the senior leadership is eager to understand each and every workers' perspective of how things are going, and how things can be improved. They talk about these issues on a daily basis, and companies from around the region sign up to study this company during monthly open house sessions. Their leaders are hungry to learn the truth, and they don't try to "push" facts down to the lower levels. This company instinctively practices the type of dialogue I've outlined and, as a consequence, is extremely strong and growing stronger every month.

When we return to the Science of Teamwork, and specifically the skills that are needed for a team to perform at its best, we find that coaching is one of the core components. According to Salas, et. al, "...coaching is necessary to recognize and help correct vital team errors or problems, as well as to provide guidance in challenging situations." Furthermore, "By recognizing the performance and process gaps that occur within a team, coaching can serve to dynamically guide and foster team development and performance throughout the team life cycle." Finally, "Perhaps the most critical role of leaders in teams that has emerged is that of diagnosing and addressing team problems as they arise."[72] The Science of Teamwork begs that this process be done in the manner outlined here.

CONCLUSION

In this chapter we've started to explore the HOW of debriefing. We've now seen a short example of the "admin debrief" and we've developed a sense for the collaborative manner in which the conversation takes place. We understand the need for some way to record what's happening in real-time so that the reconstruction of what actually took place can be accurate. We're still in the foundation stage of the debrief process, but we're moving quickly into the meat of the program. The next chapter brings us closer to that point, providing useful techniques to help you craft successful debriefs on your own.

SUMMARY

▶ The "Administrative" portion of the debrief is short but covers important subject matter.

▶ "Tape Review" is where the team members capture the facts of what happened to prepare for the debrief.

▶ In the sample dialogue, the Instructor Pilot sets the stage for psychological safety from the start, highlighting personal mistakes with just as much clarity and specificity as those of the Wingman.

▶ Debriefs facilitate coaching, which is an essentialcomponent of proper teamwork.

CHAPTER 5

PREPARING FOR A
WINNING DEBRIEF

THE SIGNIFICANT PROBLEMS WE FACE
CANNOT BE SOLVED AT THE SAME LEVEL
OF THINKING WE WERE AT WHEN WE
CREATED THEM.

Albert Einstein

*as quoted in The 7 Habits of Highly
Effective People (p. 50)*

Exercise RED FLAG is a massive aerial training event that takes place throughout the year at Nellis Air Force Base, Nevada. RED FLAG was created in 1975 as a result of our aerial combat experiences in the Vietnam War. We learned that a pilot who could survive his first 10 combat missions had a much higher chance of surviving to 100. Surviving 100 missions was critical, because getting to this number was the ticket home from Vietnam for our aircrew.

The real problem for our Vietnam-era pilots was that surviving those first 10 missions was extremely challenging. The losses we absorbed in the air war over Vietnam, while proportionally less than those in WWII or Korea, were still staggering. Red Flag's objective then and now is to get pilots past the 10-mission hump *while in the relative safety of a training environment*, before they go into combat. The core to this approach is being able to debrief these critical missions with everyone else in one huge room.

Debriefing a RED FLAG mission is a big deal. For one thing, the missions are really complex. We put our aircrew up against the most robust air-to-air and surface-to-air threats we can, in an effort to prepare them for a "worst-case" combat scenario. This ultimately means the Mission Commander—the person with the responsibility for Mission Planning, Briefing, Leading and then Debriefing the full mission—is under a LOT of pressure. For one thing, the "No-slack" environment in which our aircrew operate means that everyone who is not the Mission Commander is watching and simultaneously judging the Mission Commander's performance. Because it's the Mission Commander's job to know everything that happened, or to elicit properly those things that happened that he wasn't aware of, he has to access all available data quickly and efficiently. He has to ask the right questions at the right time, to ensure the group walks away with the correct picture of what happened, as well as the appropriate evaluation of team performance. Speaking from experience, it's an exceedingly difficult job. And it shouldn't come as a surprise that part of what enables continued success is proper preparation.

A Quick Review of Some Current Debrief Methods

Let's start with healthcare as our first brief example of an industry that practices debriefing. The Agency for Healthcare Quality and Research developed an approach to risk mitigation called TeamSTEPPS®, which has effectively become a method practiced in hospitals and healthcare clinics around the world. According to its website, TeamSTEPPS® is "A powerful solution to improving patient safety within your organization. An evidence-based teamwork system to improve communication and teamwork skills among health care professionals."[73] The approach is directly based on the way the U.S. Navy practices "Crew Resource Management," the team approach to aviation designed to minimize the potential for accidents.

TeamSTEPPS® is an incredibly powerful tool that can be applied with great success in a hospital setting. I make this claim with experience as a Patient Safety Representative at a local hospital; I've been able to see the success of this approach first-hand. That said, a typical TeamSTEPPS® debrief of a non-catastrophic mistake made in the operating room may last around 15-20 minutes. It may also require external facilitation—where someone other than those who performed the procedure is called upon to guide the debrief process. Why? Because, despite the fact that medical teams have functional leaders at the time an event takes place (say, in an operating room), the culture in the medical field doesn't necessarily maintain the same team structure *outside* the operating room. Each member of the team comes from a different background (doctors vs. nurses vs. technicians, etc.) and, critically, reports to a different leadership chain. More importantly, each member of the team is held to a slightly different standard when it comes to accountability. For example, doctors answer to peer-level reviews while nurses can be sanctioned by the hospital hierarchy. Most importantly, the focus of a TeamSTEPPS® debrief isn't directly on whether the team achieved its stated objectives. For reference, there typically are no objectives overtly stated for a given procedure. As such, the outcomes can be driven by personal attitudes, biases, hierarchical pressures and similar factors. Dominant personalities can influence outcomes. Add to this the question of just how much psychological safety is present, and participants concerned for their jobs may end up holding back important data that could affect the outcome of the debrief. In the end, the fundamental structure of the Team-STEPPS® debrief isn't designed to facilitate or grow Accountable Leadership. It's a purely functional approach designed to review issues that led to errors, and it lacks the structure to be able to repeatedly arrive at the same conclusions. Let this sink in for just a quick second and then consider the implications.

Again, there are many positives when it comes to these kinds of debriefs, and as a "client" of multiple healthcare systems I am extremely thankful we have this process in place. A quick TeamSTEPPS® debrief does allow those involved to identify areas needing improvement and can lead to finding ways to improve. It's also one of the ways healthcare systems are currently operating, and it's based on sound practice; Crew Resource Management is something I teach in my company because it's the way aviators work as a team to minimize mistakes. In my opinion, TeamSTEPPS® is a noble, science-based approach, and it's a standardized tool that allows a degree of uniformity in risk mitigation. Overall: Does it facilitate improvement? Yes. Can it be better? Of course.

The kind of change necessary to move beyond approaches like TeamSTEPPS® requires a cultural change that will take time. This cultural change would be one where every member of the medical team is held to the same standard, where teams operate as *true* teams both inside and outside of the operating room, and where functional leaders embrace their role as leaders in all areas of their work. It's a change where these functional leaders (surgeons, for example) are held appropriately accountable for their decisions and actions to the same degree as the captain of a ship or the flight lead of a fighter 4-ship. It is in our collective interest to evolve to this level, as each one of us is a client of hospitals across the globe. Getting the necessary buy-in to achieve this kind of change is the challenge we face.

It's the same with software development. A software team Retrospective (debrief) may in fact last several days. The team uses an outside facilitator to guide it through the process of determining how they've done or how they're doing. The process is not designed to build leaders, and is very different from the approach used by a high-performing team. Given the stakes at play in software design, this may well be the perfect approach—and it's certainly the way software teams are used to functioning. As such, it may be that this is the perfect plan for a given software organization, and it's clearly their call to make. What's interesting is that the Team Lifecycle Approaches used in software development have moved into other areas of business—referred to as Agile project management—and both the good and the bad of this approach have come along with it. Specifically, the Retrospective process used for software teams is also the Retrospective process now employed in other sectors of industry that are very different from software design. This has its implications on how this form of debrief is practiced, and on the lessons that derive from this particular process.

For reference, I've reviewed *Project Retrospectives* by Norman Kerth, *Agile Retrospectives: Making Good Teams Great* by Derby and Larsen, *Scrum Mastery* by Geoff Watts, along with other resources, in the interest of taking stock of what the marketplace currently offers on retrospective debriefs. I have my own copy of *Gamestorming* by Dave Gray, Sunni Brown and James Macanufo. My good friend and co-founder of *Next-Generation Edge™* is a Certified Scrum Master and globally-respected Agile Coach. We've talked at length about the state of Agile Retrospectives, and I believe that software development teams and others applying Retrospective approaches are indeed much better off because of these practices. The fact that they're debriefing in *some way* means they should be improving. I also find that Retrospective Facilitators use extremely useful techniques that can provide value early-on in a company's transition to the practice of Accountable Leadership. The techniques I find truly useful are those that help build psychological safety and help spark conversations where people might otherwise be too shy to start talking on their own.

Just like with Team-STEPPS®, the challenge with Agile Retrospectives lies in the structure. Retrospectives are not objectives-based and they don't follow a set methodology, *which means their outcomes can vary wildly.* The conclusions drawn in an Agile Retrospective are literally driven by the games the outside Facilitator chooses to play, coupled with the response these games elicit from the teams in

> UNLESS YOU ”
> FOLLOW A PROVEN
> METHODOLOGY
> THAT CENTERS ON
> THE ACHIEVEMENT
> OF OBJECTIVES
> AND ACCOUNTS
> FOR VARIED
> PERSPECTIVES, THE
> QUALITY OF THE
> DEBRIEF IS HIGHLY
> VARIABLE

question. This ultimately means that two Retrospective Facilitators might arrive at *two vastly different conclusions* at the end of a Retrospective of the *exact same event*. When it comes to building high-performing teams, this is a really big deal, and an absolutely unacceptable result. High-performing teams are really concerned with determining what went right, what didn't, and what needs to improve—centered on the objectives we set out to achieve, with the additional goal of coaching our teams to ever-greater success. The inability to replicate effective results is a challenge that Agile Retrospectives struggle with.

The point is that unless you follow a proven methodology that centers on the achievement of objectives and accounts for varied perspectives, the quality of the debrief is highly variable. This is an important consideration for companies and organizations thinking of adopting the Retrospective approach. It's an even more important consideration for those who already do so.

Setting the Stage: Preparing for a Quality Debrief

Now that we've briefly explored a couple of current approaches to debriefing, let's look at a way to set up a solid, repeatable process that any organization can replicate and use. As discussed in the previous chapter, "tape review" is a critical element of a quality debrief because in order to be effective, we need to start with the facts or the truth of what happened. It's only when we're armed with the truth that we can properly analyze if what took place was what was supposed to have taken place.

Members of the fighter pilot world have access to *a lot* of information on our tapes. My experience, especially as an Instructor Pilot, was that there was rarely enough time for a detailed tape review. I was always scrambling, trying to gather all of the data I needed in the time I was allotted, because nobody wants to show up to the debrief late. Being late is a huge foul in the fighter pilot world.

I emphasize the time challenge with tape reviews because it's the exact same in business: there will never enough time to prepare for your debriefs. Don't feel like you're alone; the best solution is to just "keep doing." By physically *"doing"*, you develop habits and techniques that enable efficiencies, and you'll figure out how to quickly capture what you really need to enable success. Learn by doing, by being active, by trying and failing, and by adopting appropriate approaches to compiling your data.

Take Notes

One of the techniques I adopted once I became an Instructor Pilot was to take notes while flying. I also occasionally spoke to myself in my tapes. I actually took notes between fights; I used my line-up card (a document with critical flight information) on my right leg and captured key details while we were setting up for the next fight. Later, during tape review, these notes would help me reconstruct what happened, as they would cue my tired brain and help me to recall specifics I might have otherwise missed. The spoken reminders in my tape served the same function.

My experience in business is almost exactly the same. I've taken to collecting notes on what's happening every day and every week, notes I later refer to in helping me to reconstruct the facts when we debrief, sometimes weeks later. Know that it is absolutely not my natural inclination to take notes every day, just like it was not a natural inclination to take notes or speak into my tapes while flying. But I find it to be an especially useful technique to help me get to the truth of what happened, something that becomes increasingly difficult with the passage of time. Because the truth of what happens is the foundation of a successful debrief, I have incorporated this approach into everything I do.

One company I work with has a scribe who captures the key points made during every meeting, whether by video conference, phone or in-person. These notes are *invaluable*, pure debrief-prep gold; they're supremely helpful in preparing for debriefing any events I lead for this company. The notes allow me to act more, record less—and still lead an extremely effective debrief.

Review Prior Performance

Something else I always did as a Flight Lead was review my Wingman's grade sheets. The purpose of the grade sheet is to both document a student's performance as well as to share performance insights with the next Instructor in the upgrade process. The insights highlight areas that require focus or additional attention. I would review these documents to determine what the student needed to work on, which in-turn helped me determine where *I* needed to take my mission briefings.

The same applies in business. Leaders should be speaking with supervisors, striving to understand their team members' individual strengths and weaknesses. This approach, of course, pre-supposes that the supervisors know their people well enough to provide these kinds of answers. These leaders are then better poised to lead "mission briefings" tailored to their audiences, with a focus on items that require emphasis. This, then, also feeds into how we structure the debrief. If we focus on a particular subject in the briefing, specifically because it was an area of concern on the previous "grade sheet," we also focus on the same subject in the debrief to emphasize whether or not we achieved the progress we were looking for. It just makes sense.

Self-Reflection

We saw this in action in the earlier example, when the Instructor Pilot offered a critical assessment of his own performance in the debrief. The self-reflection process usually begins during tape review and carries on throughout the debrief. In fact, it's critical that what we'll soon identify as a "Level 3 Leader" continuously self-reflects throughout the debrief to arrive at the most correct conclusions. Taking the time to self-reflect and measure one's performance against expectations and established Standards, Tactics and Checklists is critical for a productive, honest debrief.

My approach to doing this correctly was always to review in my mind's eye everything I did, from planning through execution, assessing whether or not I met my own performance expectations. When the answer was "no", I wrote down the issue and made a mental note to ensure I offered a "fix" in my ensuing discussion. By the way, highlighting a problem in a fighter debrief without offering a "fix" is unacceptable.

The same applies in a business setting. In fact, a frustration I've picked up on from my work around the country is that inside organizations that do actually conduct some form of debrief, often the process ends once the Root Cause of a fault is determined (shockingly, most organizations don't take the time to determine Root Causes of successes). Team members have shared with me the challenge of going through a debrief-style process to figure out why something went wrong, and then ending up without any associated action. Functionally, this sort of process serves no purpose. Unless we identify an appropriate fix—which is essentially our hypothesis of how we can do better next time around—we've *wasted our time* debriefing. Much more on this in a bit.

Visualization

Finally, I cannot overstate the importance of pre-mission visualization, both for mission preparation and debrief preparation. On nights prior to a big mission, I would routinely visualize how I would craft and lead my debrief to success. I envisioned how I planned to handle difficult personalities, how

I was going to remain focused on the mission-critical items, how I was going to keep the team centered on the objectives (and not get diverted), and *how I was going to end the debrief on an extremely positive note*. Taking the time to visualize all of this made the debrief execution feel more natural. This allowed me to be much more up-beat during the debrief than I might have otherwise been—which in turn helped me focus more on the substance.

I learned this approach all the way back in pilot training, where we acted on this process of visualization through what we called "chair flying." We would literally sit in our chairs and simulate radio calls, muscle movements (reaching for switches, controls, etc.), and visual lookout practices, helping us to develop comfort with new habit patterns. It turns out that science justifies this approach completely. According to psychiatrist and author, Dr. Abigail Brenner, "The subconscious mind is a programmable 'hard drive'. The 'programs' of our lives, which are largely stimulus-response behaviors, are downloaded into our subconscious. The subconscious does not rely on the outside world for its 'knowing,' and so it can't differentiate between what is real and what is imagined. The subconscious remembers everything, is absolutely literal (which means there's no subtlety), and processes only in the present tense. It will look for and guide you to whatever you tell it." Given this knowledge, Dr. Brenner goes on to explain the approach we must take: "You must be absolutely clear and specific in directing your subconscious to help you accomplish your goals. The subconscious mind uses imagination and feeling to communicate; you can practice in your mind without ever doing the actions."[74] There is no doubt in my mind that visualizing a successful debrief will pay tremendous dividends during the process, especially when you're leading one of these events the first few times. I still visualize my debriefs—especially in the consulting world—to this very day, to great success, and highly recommend it.

Understanding the Context

Of the many critical elements that produce a high quality debrief, context is one of the most important. By context, we're talking about "What kind of debrief is this?" Is this an "upgrade ride," one where the student is working to earn an advanced qualification, such as upgrading from Wingman to Flight Lead? Is this a "Continuation Training" ride, where the team is working on maintaining proficiency, but where there is no grade sheet to fill out at the end? Is this a combat mission where time is short, and where our Intelligence team needs to know more than anything what we saw / experienced / heard / felt during flight to help us better prepare for tomorrow? Is this a cross-country deployment where we're simply moving airplanes from one place to another? In the business world, is this an evaluation to assess how the employee is performing in comparison to established standards? Is this a team performance review where we're looking at team progress in comparison to stated objectives and completion timelines?

The context tells me up-front roughly how much time the debrief is going to take. For example, and upgrade ride will *usually* involve a more comprehensive debrief than a Continuation Training ride debrief. This is not an absolute, but it's a starting point. And a cross-country debrief is almost always a very quick debrief.

More important than the timing, the context sets the stage for the level of analysis. If I am an Instructor Pilot on an upgrade mission, my focus is to both *evaluate* my student's performance on all phases of the mission: mission planning, briefing, in-flight execution, and debriefing, and then to *coach or instruct* him or her on ways to improve. For example, if my student is learning how to become what we call a 4-Ship Flight Lead, she will plan, brief, lead and debrief the 4-ship—that is, the full team. Her focus is on making sure she debriefs everyone in the formation—to include myself as the Instructor, to standards. Then, once she's finished with her debrief, I get to address any points I need to make to the group (correcting anything that was done or said incorrectly, and addressing any gaps I identified). I then excuse the other members of the formation and debrief the student on her planning, briefing, leadership and debriefing. This is what typically makes these debriefs last longer than others.

On the other hand, if we're on a Continuation Training mission, the focus is more on standards adherence, tactical execution and ways we as a team can get better. As the Flight lead, I will debrief our combined performance and then allow team members to get on with planning for tomorrow. In BOTH cases the focus is on improvement; the question is only where the emphasis comes into play.

Debrief Structure: Who Leads?

One of the problems with Accountable Leadership in the business world is that we don't train our leaders to lead in an accountable manner. We train managers to manage because that's really easy, but we don't train young leaders to lead by holding themselves and their team members accountable. We sidestep this, largely because we're afraid others won't accept us or will see us as "mean." We avoid conflict because we're afraid of the implications and our status. We want to be loved, and we want our followers to think well of us. The funny thing is that people *want* to be led. They want to work for accountable leaders; they're starved of good leadership! Ask yourself what you think about these statements. My guess is you agree.

When addressing who leads the debrief, we're really getting to the crux of one of the problems in corporations across the globe: how do we train our future leaders to be accountable? The answer from the world of high-performing teams is easy: have your current and future leaders lead their team debriefs! And you should set your organization's example by leading your own debriefs.

As a young Captain, I debriefed generals. I knew my craft well enough to speak the truth during the debrief—in a respectful and appropriate way, of course. But I absolutely held my leadership accountable for their decisions and actions, as I did every other member of the team. In fact, my leaders *expected* me to do this. And in order to do so, I had to be ready,

I had to be qualified and I had to be empowered. Our training ensured that I was all three, and I learned, at a very early age, how to lead the people who eventually led our Air Force. As the Mission Commander for all U.S. forces involved in Operation SOUTHERN WATCH on September 12, 2001—which of course occurred right on the heels of the terrorist atrocities that forever changed our world—I led the future head of Air Combat Command, at the time a 1-star general who would retire with 4 stars...and I was only a Captain, four short years removed from pilot training.

In the fighter pilot world, the Flight Lead leads the debrief, regardless of rank, experience or comfort level. The theory holds that the privilege of leading a formation of high-performance fighter aircraft—whether in training or combat—is accompanied by the responsibility of being in charge of the accountability process. The Flight Lead's leadership responsibility does not end until the conclusion of the debrief. This re-emphasizes the leadership role of the Flight Lead, and drives leadership development in young Flight Leads at a very early stage.

I've noted that this can be a touchy subject in the business world, especially in organizations where the concept of the formal debrief is a new practice. The leader of the debrief ultimately assigns direct responsibility for performance issues; he or she also highlights and publicly praises whoever it was that enabled mission success. In organizations where such an accountability practice is new, and where the culture has to adjust to practice accountability in this way, people might feel more comfortable bringing in a debrief consultant. This crutch can be a very useful tool and might even become a company's status-quo—which, by the way, is why I disagree with the approach from the start.

If a company is eager to advance its practice of Accountable Leadership, leaders need to begin by practicing public accountability. Leaders should lead the debrief. The idea of bringing in an outsider to lead the debrief—as is often done in the world of healthcare or software development—can help deflect criticism and protect functional leaders. The critical assumption is that the debrief facilitator knows enough about what they're doing to lead an effective debrief, an assumption that can be flawed from the outset. My question is this: what makes an outside facilitator qualified to lead *your* debrief? What do they know about your team, your processes, your values and ethos, and your goals that makes them more qualified than you to lead your team?

> ❝ LEADERS SHOULD LEAD THE DEBRIEF

The main problem with this approach is that outsourcing accountability means we remain stuck in a world where we aren't growing accountable leaders. In fact, this approach perpetuates the problem. I'm stunned that companies do this so frequently. I know the external facilitators are doing so with the best of intent and are working to bring value. I also believe that they're applying the approaches they know to the best of their abilities, and that good can come of this. But this is at best an incredibly inefficient approach to building accountable leaders *as well as followers* in an organization that wants to be the best.

Debrief Structure: Who Else Participates?

The next question is, "who besides the Leader participates?" The good news is that the answer is easy: everyone who has a stake. If in doubt, be more inclusive. The rationale is simple— to have access to the truth, everyone who has a perspective of that truth has to be present. Do not undervalue the importance of a perspective, even from a member of the team you think to be insignificant. I've seen instances where the person others thought the least of (in terms of their value to the debrief) had the most powerful or important perspective of the truth, which led to a game-changing conclusion.

In addition, filling in for, or speaking on behalf of, someone not present is a recipe for team disaster. I've seen situations where the one person who didn't make it to the debrief was up in arms after reading the debrief summary. They felt mis-represented and took the conclusions, the "fix" as we'll come to know it, as a false indictment—targeted against them. They took offense at a very non-controversial outcome, because they ended up taking the conclusions personally. I've watched a good person (with little debrief experience) momentarily lose his mind over this, which was equal parts comical and frustrating. Again: everyone who has a stake in what's happened should be in the debrief.

The degree of participation demonstrates just how important the company or organization holds the debrief to be. In those organizations where few people who were part of the planning, briefing and executing attend the debrief, it becomes clear that neither the participants, nor the leaders themselves, consider the debrief to be all that important. They disrespect the debrief process. Conversely, in organizations where debrief attendance is mandatory and leadership follows-up on who participates and how involved they are, it becomes very clear how important the debrief is. Organizations that get this right—that take the debrief seriously and use it as an effective tool for growth—benefit in ways that might shock the uninitiated. According to the team at DebriefNow, research proves "that debriefs help teams establish effective norms, build trust and confidence and decrease subsequent decision-making time—and are among the most efficient means of building and ensuring team effectiveness."[75]

Debriefing Rules of Engagement

Assuming everybody shows up for the debrief, the leader's first challenge is gaining and maintaining control of what can often be seen as "the crowd." Where there are many voices to be heard, there can be much wasted conversation. Powerful personalities can dominate the process, especially in organizations that aren't used to conducting debriefs. These strong personalities can even make the debrief almost pointless. The best way to address this is to implement Debrief Rules of Engagement (ROE). These should include, at a minimum, the following points:

▶ Nobody speaks unless recognized (i.e. approved) by the leader;

▶ Nobody is allowed to jump to conclusions—give the process room to work;

▶ Nobody gets to play "I've got a secret"—if you have a key piece of data, share it;

▶ Don't let the leader go down a path he or she shouldn't— help the leader stay on-track;

▶ Everyone acknowledges they're here to find ways to improve.

In addition, the Leader should set the conditions for success by pre-briefing the team to help them understand the process. Team members need complete clarification as to when they have a speaking part and when they don't. In most cases, your teammates will not understand this, and will unwittingly hijack your debrief as a result. One way to prevent this is to implement a short debrief training program prior to your first debrief to help set the stage for success.

The leader needs to begin the process by formalizing the ROE—and creating a "Team Charter" is a really powerful means of doing this. This is where the team agrees on operating parameters before they start the debrief. One technique I like is to have a rule where you can't talk unless you're both recognized and are holding the "coffee mug 'o justice." Another useful technique is issuing a penalty for speaking when not recognized. The Team Charter consists of codifying whatever rules the team thinks they'll need in order to move forward in a safe and productive manner. This is highly dependent on the composition of the team, the industry, and the degree of comfort with debriefs. Additionally, Norman Kerth, in his book *Project Retrospectives*, suggests using what he calls a "Prime Directive". His example of such a directive reads:

> *Regardless of what we discover, we understand and truly believe that everyone did the best job they could, given what they knew at the time, their skills and abilities, the resources available, and the situation at hand.*[76]

Setting your company or organization up to make the transition is critical, and these are two quick and simple techniques to enable adoption. Most importantly, it's critical to hold each other accountable for rule violations. A Team Charter means nothing if the people responsible fail to uphold the standards.

LEADERSHIP HIGHLIGHT

Debrief decorum. Maintaining control of the crowd while leading this process can be a challenge, especially with "seasoned veterans" in the room. I led one such event a few months ago and those who had the most experience in business tended to try to leap ahead or offer their thoughts on what they had decided we all needed to know. The problem was that these comments weren't helping—and were actually diluting the debrief process. It's important to set expectations up front, as previously mentioned, and then to keep control as the leader, stopping such chatter immediately, potentially with a fun repercussion.

- Requires preparation from the Flight Lead;

- Requires adherence to debrief standards, maybe a Team Charter and perhaps a Prime Directive;

- Requires a conversation with the team prior to the debrief.

This part takes practice, and some getting used to.

How Long Will the Debrief Last?

Here's a little peek into the world of fighter pilot instructors: by-far the most popular answer offered by an Instructor Pilot to any question is, "It depends." It also happens to be the truth, as there are few absolutes in extremely complex operating environments. And when it comes to the question of how long a debrief will last, I'll offer it this perfect answer as your Debrief IP: "It depends."

As noted, much is decided by context, and the gravity of the events that took place help shape the timing. If, for example, I was flying a Continuation Training mission with a fellow Instructor Pilot that went according to plan, the debrief might be as short as 30-60 minutes. If, on the other hand, I was flying on an "Upgrade" ride where a young pilot was qualifying for a new status, we might spend a few hours in our debrief.

When executed by seasoned practitioners, corporate debriefs can be completed in an extremely efficient manner. According to Reyes, Tannenbaum and Salas, an effective business debrief can take place in 15-60 minutes.[77] What matters most, however, is not the timing, but the effectiveness of the process. I'm emphatic about this: *by emphasizing effectiveness over timing the debrief will become the most useful tool in your leadership and teamwork kit.* And the only way to have effective, efficient debriefs is to practice, practice and practice the art of debriefing. Few things come easy, and skill in debriefing requires dedicated effort, coupled with focused training and, likely, coaching.

The 4 Levels of Results Analysis

It's probably become obvious to you as we explore this process that many organizations incorporate *components* of debriefs in their work. Some of the best businesses do take the time to measure performance against objectives to improve results. The problem I've consistently seen is that well-meaning companies simply don't have the methodologies to get beyond justifying why there's a gap between desired and actual performance. I've therefore developed the following scale to help companies identify where they are in terms of debrief sophistication:

▶   **Level 0:** No Organized Reviews or Debriefs

▶ **Level 1:** An Organized Review ending in Explanation / Justification (Basic "Why")

▶ **Level 2:** Debrief-Level Analysis with first-step Root Cause Determination (Root Cause analysis)

▶ **Level 3:** Full Debrief-Level Analysis: practice of Accountable Leadership with second-step *Root Cause Determination (Leadership Impact)*

Level 0 is the easiest to describe; as a company that simply doesn't formally review performance. They do what they do based on gut feel, instinct and "seat-of-the pants" assessments. Though organizations may stumble upon success despite this approach, luck is not a strategy.

Level 1 Analysis is where many companies arrive with good intentions…and find themselves stuck. These organizations are outstanding at highlighting both the negative and positive gaps in performance (it's always fun to highlight outstanding performance), but can't move much beyond justification of the results. In Level 1 debriefs, leaders say something like "We were 12 units shy of our objective. The reason is that Brian didn't contact enough prospects. Next month, Brian is going to target all of his prospects." Such an answer is often considered sufficient because organizations don't know any better, and companies—especially those experiencing success— feel comfortable living in a Level 1 kind of world. But we're missing the answers to the critical questions, such as *why* Brian didn't contact enough prospects. We should be asking whether his workload is too high, whether he's using the proper sales pitch, whether he's approaching the right prospects, whether he's using his time effectively, etc. We need substantive answers instead of surface-level justifications.

Level 1 debriefs, while perhaps slightly uncomfortable for the leader highlighting a negative gap, are nice because they're usually really quick. Most critically, when teams get into a rhythm of briefing the same basic results every month / quarter / year and the justified results are deemed sufficient; these are very comfortable debriefs. This last point is why Level 1 debriefs are entirely insufficient for companies and organizations that want to excel, that want to go from "Good to Great."

Level 2 and Level 3 Analysis

Level 2 Analysis gets to the real Root Cause of why team members either did or did not meet their objectives. It's never just because Brian didn't contact enough prospects; it's never just Brian not doing his full job. Level 2 debriefs look at all of the components that affected performance. They utilize implicit or formal techniques like "Five Why's" (Toyota Production System), "Fishbone" or "Ishikawa Diagrams" (Kawasaki), and similar techniques. The point is that the first answer we arrive at is usually insufficient; we need to do more probing to arrive at a Root Cause we will eventually accept. Returning to our friend Brian, we would be analyzing why it was that

Brian didn't speak to enough contacts. We would keep on asking "Why?" until the answer we drilled down to was more than reasonable; it would be the correct answer which, when addressed, would ensure that Brian will accomplish the necessary activity to achieve the desired results.

Level 3 Analysis takes this approach to the next, most appropriate level. This is where the leader self-evaluates and determines what impact his or her planning, briefing and decision-making had on the results. The Level 2 debrief may indeed point to an appropriate answer, but a Level 3 addition is often the absolute truth—one where we determine that the Leader's poor planning, poor communication, and/or poor decision-making that ultimately led to the failure. Returning briefly to Brian, his leader would question whether he or she set the conditions for Brian's success—whether he received adequate training, whether the leader developed a good or thorough enough plan for Brian to follow. The leader would be looking for gaps *in his or her own leadership and performance* that may account for Brian's error.

Fans of Jim Collins' bestselling book *Good to Great* might notice that Level 3 Analysis links directly to what Collins identifies as a "Level 5 Leader—an individual who blends extreme personal humility with intense professional will." Most importantly, "Level 5 leaders channel their ego needs away from themselves and into the larger goal of building a great company...they are incredibly ambitious—*but their ambition is first and foremost for the institution, not themselves.*" By focusing on the good of the institution, a Level 5 leader can apply a Level 3 Analysis to their own personal performance, identifying and publicly sharing those areas in which they failed to help their teams be all they can be. Level 5 leaders never stop trying to be their best, and never stop working to demonstrate why they're in the leadership position they're in. To emphasize this point, Collins shares the following comment from Darwin Smith, former CEO of Kimberly-Clark, and the reason for Kimberly-Clark's staggering success from 1971 to 1991, "I never stopped trying to become qualified for the job."[78] Practicing Level 3 Analysis through properly-run debriefs helps keep leaders on the Level 5 track, which is a great thing for the organization at all levels.

Foot Stomp: Decisions vs. Outcomes

Let's briefly discuss the critical difference between decisions and outcomes. In fact, these few short paragraphs will highlight an issue that deserves its own chapter. Making high quality decisions is essential to any organization's success. However, the fact that an individual or team made a good decision doesn't necessarily mean that the outcome will be good. Many factors are at play when it comes to outcomes, and the only thing the organization (and really, the leadership) has any control over is the quality of the decision, especially in complex situations. We can state with certainty that making a good decision is almost always better than making a bad one. On the other side of the equation is what happens as a result of that decision—and we always face the problem that bad decisions can still result in good outcomes, and good outcomes can be achieved by luck. Good decisions can also result in bad outcomes, which is why we don't want to focus exclusively on the bad outcome and immediately lament the decision. What matters, really, is whether or not we're making good decisions, and whether our leaders are facilitating the development of good decisions.

One challenge when we look at the quality of our decisions is that we inherently equate good outcomes or results with quality decisions. Though instinctive, this is a poor approach. World-class poker player Annie Duke, in her brilliant book *Thinking in Bets*, highlights this problem in what she refers to as "resulting." She writes, "... resulting is a routine thinking pattern that bedevils all of us. Drawing an overly tight relationship between results and decision quality affects our decisions every day, potentially with far-reaching, catastrophic consequences."[79] On a related note she highlights, "Hindsight bias is the tendency, after an outcome is known, to see the outcome as having been inevitable. When we say, 'I should have known that would happen,' or 'I should have seen it coming,' we are succumbing to hindsight bias."[80]

> IF WE AREN'T WRONG JUST BECAUSE THINGS DIDN'T WORK OUT, THEN WE AREN'T RIGHT JUST BECAUSE THINGS TURNED OUT WELL

Back when I was an instructor at the Weapons School, I "busted" (our terminology for "failed") a student on a mission where the outcome was exactly what we wanted. We achieved mission success; we hit all of our objectives; and, from an outsider's point of view, we did very well. The only problem was that our debrief demonstrated clearly that the outcome was not a result of the decisions we made in flight. The fact was that we just got lucky. My reason for "busting" the student was to highlight that, on another day, against another adversary, a repeat of our decisions would not likely achieve the same positive outcome. The student wasn't happy, but this is how we approach missions at the Weapons School. This is also the conceptual background that takes us to Level 2 and 3 debriefs, those that promote excellence in decision-making.

Rest-assured, the flip is also true—I passed people on missions that didn't end well because the quality of the decisions and in-flight leadership was good. In summary, Ms. Duke notes, "Redefining wrong allows us to let go of all the anguish that comes from getting a bad result. But it also means we must redefine 'right.' If we aren't wrong just because things didn't work out, then we aren't right just because things turned out well."[81] Again, there is a lot here, and I highly recommend learning more about this by reading *Thinking in Bets*.

Basic Debrief Setup

The first step in any effective debrief is being prepared. This means ensuring the room is set the way it needs to be and there are spaces for every member of the team. If we're going to use technology, we make sure all required systems work in advance. If we plan to use whiteboards, chalk boards or butcher boards, we have functioning markers, chalk or pens and we have enough space to get the job done. I highly recommend whiteboards or butcher boards. Accurately keeping track of team inputs is going to be instrumental to your success. The debrief process is iterative, and unless there's a way for the leader to quickly and correctly capture the key points in a way that everyone can also see them, embrace them, think on them and use them for good, the process can suffer.

We come armed with a visual depiction of our objectives. Ideally these are written on a board, where they were during the pre-mission briefing. Next, we make sure that everyone who needs to be present knows where the debrief is going to be held and at what time—perhaps an e-mail invite best addresses this need. Our teammates are aware that we expect them to be both present and mentally ready to contribute; if certain teammates need to bring specific items to the debrief, they also know about this in advance. Along with this, we're ready to ask for "Alibis"—that is, things that came about after the plan was briefed that clearly affected someone's ability to execute as planned. For example, I may have had to fly an airplane where the RADAR didn't work, which limited my ability to find enemy aircraft. It is good to note these problems up-front, so that we don't waste any time exploring why I didn't execute my portion of the plan. Alibis help us focus based on the reality we dealt with in execution. The same basic practice applies to all debriefs in business and life. Finally, we're prepared to provide a quick summary of the plan we intended to execute. It's important to kick off the debrief with a re-cap of the plan to remind people—especially if there's a significant delay between execution and debrief. To summarize:

▶ We prominently display our objectives;

▶ We make sure everyone knows when and where the debrief will take place, as well as what everyone's responsibilities are;

▶ We are prepared to discuss our "Alibis"

▶ We provide a summary of the plan we intended to execute, a quick overview of where we intended to start and how we planned to move forward.

CONCLUSION

In this chapter we introduced the first details on "the how" of debriefing. We discussed how best to prepare, to include techniques to help develop an accurate Reconstruction. We described reflection and visualization techniques, as well as outlined how context drives timing and level of analysis. We also covered decision quality in comparison to outcomes, and recommended the book *Thinking in Bets* by Annie Duke as a useful resource. We offered granularity in setting up the debrief and discussed roles and responsibilities, the importance of Rules of Engagement and the "4 Levels of Results

Analysis." In short, we set the stage for what's to come by providing the setup and mental preparation requirements for a high-quality fighter-style debrief. In the next chapter we'll explore the specific debrief methodology that allows us to truly *Debrief to Win*.

SUMMARY

▶ Setting the stage: debriefs require preparation

▶ Part of the preparation for a good debrief involves taking notes

▶ An outstanding practice is to prepare by reviewing previous performance, where possible

▶ Good debrief leadership requires self-reflection

▶ A winning debrief involves visualization

▶ Context defines the parameters of a debrief

▶ Different circumstances influence how detailed a debrief will be

▶ Other kinds of debriefs can achieve good results, but have variable outcomes and aren't consistent

▶ Leaders should lead the debrief

- ▶ Everyone involved in a given event should participate in the debrief

- ▶ Debriefs should start with Rules of Engagement

- ▶ Debrief length depends on a number of variables

- ▶ There are 4 levels of Results Analysis

- ▶ We're looking at the quality of decisions made vs. the outcomes achieved

- ▶ Level 2 and 3 debriefs are what we're striving for in high-performing organizations

- ▶ The basic structure and setup of the debrief is effectively a checklist

CHAPTER 6

THE "RAPTOR" DEBRIEF

66

FAILURE IS INSTRUCTIVE. THE PERSON
WHO REALLY THINKS LEARNS QUITE AS
MUCH FROM HIS FAILURES FROM
HIS SUCCESSES.

John Dewey

Overview

I was blessed in my career with being able to fly both the F-15
"Eagle" and the F-22 "Raptor," both absolutely outstanding aircraft. I became an Instructor and Evaluator Pilot in the "Eagle,"

and taught expert "Eagle" employment at the Weapons School. A little later on, I was privileged to be able to command a Raptor unit, where I led the outstanding men and women of the 7th Fighter Squadron. While my heart will forever remain with the Eagle (it's a truly magnificent machine, one that I consider myself extremely fortunate to have been deemed worthy enough to fly), the Raptor is a manifestation of the absolute best that current defense industry can produce, the same as the Eagle was in its day. The Raptor represents a technological leap in capability over the Eagle and performs brilliantly on every stage. Aside from its cost (approximately $154M per copy) and the related fact that our government only purchased 187 of these aircraft (far too few to replace the largely-retired Eagle inventory), in the Raptor our Air Force has a capability that is truly unparalleled.

I was extremely blessed to command a Raptor squadron, and the Raptor was the last military aircraft I ever flew. I'll therefore return to my time in the 7th Fighter Squadron for the naming convention we'll use to help us learn the mechanics of the debrief: The *RAPTOR Debrief.*

What's critical, and truly powerful about the RAPTOR Debrief methodology is that it's both simple and repeatable. Every debrief should have exactly the same structure. It's also critical to note that *each component can be practiced by every member of the team—from senior leaders and managers, all the way down to technicians and lower-level workers.* Importantly, the RAPTOR Debrief is not only a tool for high-performing teams to hold themselves accountable; it's a life skill that applies in ALL areas of human endeavor. Know that the six steps we'll outline here are designed to be:

1. *Simple to understand,*

2. *Easy to implement, and*

3. *Immensely powerful when used correctly.*

A quick observation on the structure of this chapter: we're now shifting to an explanation of how to *implement* the specific steps of the debrief—steps that build on everything else we've covered in the book thus far. A good way to approach this chapter is as if you were a student in a business training course. I'm going to identify how you can use these six steps for personal and organizational gain, which means that I'll be offering a relatively academic approach in the coming pages. My recommendation is that you get a notepad and a highlighter. Be prepared to reflect on certain passages and connect the dots between the components and how you can use them to your benefit. Highlight the sections that either don't make sense now, or that help the light bulb come on—in terms of how to apply them to meet your needs. Take notes and reflect on them. Come back to them. Don't let them gather dust in a forgotten notebook. And if you have questions that the book doesn't address, please feel free to write me directly. My *Debrief to Win* e-mail address is **feedback@debrieftowin.com.** My goal is to provide an appropriate and meaningful answer to your questions within a reasonable amount of time, usually a matter of days, and to use your questions to help refine future editions of this book. With that, here's how we're going to use the RAP-TOR Debrief to efficiently and correctly improve ourselves and our organizations:

Step 1: Reconstruct What Happened

As I noted in Chapter 5, those of us in the flying world employ technology devoted to helping us reconstruct exactly what happened while airborne. The purpose is to ensure that we have precise "truth data" from which to extract our lessons. Whether we realize it or not, we have many of those same capabilities in business. Every company to whom I've provided consulting services is able to capture very accurate numbers on sales performance and other key metrics. Metrics are an excellent way of capturing *one component* of the "truth data" we seek, as the numbers themselves are only one aspect of what needs to be captured during the "Reconstruction" phase.

What's even more important is that we have an accurate capture of ALL of the key events / occurrences / statistics / etc. that affected our performance. It's critical that we marry the different perspectives of what these looked like from the standpoint of the various members of our team. I'll use our dogfighting example from Chapter 4 to demonstrate what I mean, and how we apply this approach in a fighter debrief.

The Tactical Debrief

You'll recall, that the Flight Lead in our "dogfight" example finished the administrative portion of the debrief and transitioned to the tactical part of the mission, "the meat" of the mission. The first thing he needs to do is to ensure both pilots agree on what actually happened. He'll do this by reconstructing the path each fighter flew. He'll place special emphasis on times when the Offensive Fighter employed weapons, as well as those times where the two might have had a close pass, and where one was able to gain an advantage over the other. The challenge with manually reconstructing the flight paths of high-performance fighters is that what actually transpired in the air did so in three dimensions. The simplest forms of reconstruction—chalk boards, white boards, butcher boards—only allow for a two-dimensional reconstruction. That said, we always train to manually draw up our engagements because we thereby learn how to ask critical questions of our teammates.

To assist in our manual reconstruction, the Flight Lead will initially reconstruct the fight from what we call the "God's-eye" perspective: as you might imagine, looking straight down from the heavens. The other perspective we use is the "Grandstand" perspective, where the fight is viewed as if from the bleachers or grandstand at a sports event.

My main purpose in this example is to highlight how the Flight Lead talks out loud during the Reconstruction phase, regularly gathering, depicting, and confirming data with his Wingman. The better the data capture, the more accurate the reconstruction, and the Flight Lead (FL) is centered on capturing accurate data. The only way to guarantee accuracy is to ask lots of pointed questions. There is no doubt who's in charge during the Reconstruction phase of the fighter debrief, and who is providing the source data against which everything is checked. But there's also no escaping the fact that the Wingman (WG) has important information to add—a perspective of the event that has to be captured for the reconstruction to be accurate. The process I'm trying to describe typically looks something like this, in the "God's-eye" perspective:

A Sample Reconstruction

*Please realize I am not trying to teach you how to debrief a fighter mission here. I'm also not trying to get you to debrief to this particular standard, or level of detail. Rather, I'm illustrating an example of the process that helps us quickly arrive at the truth. Please read this short section only to gain an appreciation for the questioning process used to arrive at the facts—and I promise we'll see how this applies in a practical, non-aviation example shortly.

FL: *OK, on our first engagement I'm showing you in a right-hand turn and at the "Fight's-on" you're heading approximately 040 degrees. Can you confirm your heading, as well as your airspeed at the Fight's-on?*

WG: *Absolutely. I'm heading 037 degrees and I'm at 376 knots.*

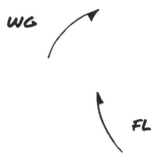

Figure 1: Each line represents the forward movement of a jet, the relative position of each jet to the other, and reflects a turning flight (positive G's)

FL: *Perfect. What I'll see from you is that you immediately go into what looks like a level tighten-down, as my nose starts to pull out In lead of you. Do you see my nose rotating out in lead? And do you indeed do a level tighten-down?*

WG: *Yes, I'm tightening down mostly level and as I'm watching you over my right shoulder I see your nose rapidly moving out in lead.*

FL: *OK, good. I'm tightening from the 'Fight's-on' and am bleeding off my airspeed in the process. Right about the time I'm approaching a gun solution I'm down to 365 knots. I watch as your airplane rotates, and you quickly escape with what looks to me to be a vertical jink. It looks like you start this jink at a heading of roughly 140 degrees, and it looks to me like a pure vertical maneuver. Is this indeed what you do?*

163

WG: Exactly. I feel threatened and I decide that my best
        option is to do a vertical jink to spoil your shot and
        to change the fight a bit. I enter at a heading of 135
        degrees and start pulling.

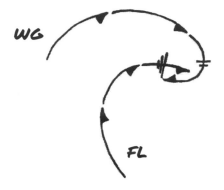

Figure 2: Here we see three "time slices" of movement. Ultimately,
the wingman starts moving "into" the page, indicated by the
shorthand: ⟩ and the flight lead starts climbing, as indicated by
the shorthand: ✦

FL: OK. Can you tell me your altitude and airspeed at the
        point where you begin your jink?

WG: Yep...I'm at 17.5 thousand feet and I'm at 342 knots.

At this point you should understand what I'm trying to describe to you. We draw the lines on our board while we're gathering information, asking important questions and validating
that the information we have is as accurate as possible. We'll
often find that we've made mistakes along the way—during
the rush of tape review we might have copied data incorrectly,

missed information or somehow misled ourselves. If we can't figure it out between the two of us we'll return to the tapes, the truth data itself, and try again. The point is that at the end of this process we can look at the board to gain an extremely accurate depiction of what happened, so that we can then focus the debrief on those things that really warrant our attention. If we don't go through this process, we might each have our own different perspective of what actually took place. If we start our analysis with different versions of the truth, we set ourselves up to arrive at erroneous conclusions.

Reconstructing in a Business Setting

When it comes to reconstructing events that took place on the ground, and which may have taken place over many days, weeks and even years—fear not. The same basic methodology works.

It is just as achievable to execute a "tape review" by all participants to capture individual perspectives of key events, as well as to undergo a Reconstruction phase where those key events are listed on a board for all to see. We don't have tapes in the business context, of course; so, we use memory, e-mails and text messages, our notes, data spreadsheets and whatever else we use to capture information to help us reconstruct what actually took place. The key to success here is to combine clarity and brevity.

For example, let's say we have a driver transporting concrete—a substance that can only be kept tumbling for so long before it's unusable. He is delayed en route, and has been asked to perform a reconstruction of his challenges with a few quick notes. In doing so, he might capture the instructions he was issued, the route he took, his experiences along the route, the decisions he made based on the challenges he encountered, and end with the actual time it took him to get from point A to B. The process might look something like this:

* DESTINATION ADDRESS PROVIDED BY MANAGEMENT AT 6 AM, NO SPECIAL INSTRUCTIONS GIVEN

* ADDRESS ENTERED INTO ON-BOARD GPS AT 6:05 AM; DID NOT CHECK MY TRAFFIC APP FOR TRAFFIC PATTERNS EN ROUTE

* DEPARTED HQ AT 6:08 AM VIA I-25N

* ~30 MINUTES INTO TRIP, WHILE ON I-25, TRAFFIC WAS BROUGHT TO A STANDSTILL BECAUSE OF CONSTRUCTION—THE ENTIRE NORTH-BOUND SIDE OF HIGHWAY WAS SHUT DOWN

* AT 7:53 I WAS FINALLY ABLE TO EXIT HIGHWAY AT PEAK STREET, A TOTAL OF 1.2 MILES TOWARDS DESTINATION

* TRAFFIC ON PEAK STREET WAS BACKED-UP DUE TO TRAFFIC FLOW COUPLED WITH ALL OF THE HIGHWAY TRAFFIC SPILLING OUT DUE TO THE CONSTRUCTION

* **A SUBSEQUENT TRAFFIC JAM CAUSED BY AN ACCIDENT LED TO A 40-MINUTE HALT ON BAY STREET**

* **ONCE THE ACCIDENT CLEARED, IT TOOK 3 HOURS 52 MINUTES TO ARRIVE AT THE DESTINATION**

This is a clear capture of all the key data points and helps paint the picture of what actually took place on a challenging day. Armed with this information, the opportunity to figure out WHY this driver experienced these challenges becomes clear. Capturing the data in short sentences is an outstanding and productive way to move forward.

A Visual Capture of the Truth of What Happened

What's especially useful is that having the truth *in print* in front of us, prompts the problems we want to solve—and the answers to these problems—to jump straight out, especially if we're thinking critically. This is not to say that the answers are directly written on the board—often they're not. But if we've got the truth right, and we as leaders are always looking at the problem through the lens of, "Did I set my team up for success?" we can quickly figure out what we need to know to achieve success.

I used this approach while working with a client several months ago. In this particular case we were debriefing a special event we hosted which combined elements from all parts of the company (marketing and sales, operations, finance, etc.), as well as introduced an emerging non-profit entity to the world. I specifically captured the events that took place over the course of three weeks on one piece of flip chart paper as part of our debrief. I divided our reconstruction in weekly chunks, and further sub-divided the reconstruction into components that made sense to our team. These components included "Management Team", "Events", "Sales" and an additional sub-group. I also added a category called "Pressure Points" which were areas that gave us difficulties along the way. Here's what the end result of this particular Reconstruction looked like:

> **PRE-EVENT #1**
EVENTS THAT PRE-EXISTED CURRENT PROGRAM

> **WEEK 1**

MGT TEAM: FOCUS WAS ON ORGANIZATIONAL DEVELOPMENT
EVENTS: BUILDING A PLAN + ASSIGNING ROLES
SALES: REFINE PROJECT + SALES ARE
FOUNDATION: UNDERSTAND THE FULL-SCOPE
PRESSURE POINTS: BUDGETS / EXPECTATIONS / LEGAL

> **WEEK 2**

MGT TEAM: CONTINUE ABOVE / DRUM-BEAT / PRIOIRITIES
*EVENTS: ACTION ON PLANNING / FULFILLING NEW DUTIES
SALES: AWAITING WORDS ON LICENSE
        UNCLEAR ON RELATIONSHIPS + HOW TO SPEAK
        BUILDING PROJECT + SPONSORSHIP
FOUNDATION: AWAITING FURTHER INSTRUCTIONS
PRESSURE POINTS: RESOURCE CONSTRAINTS
                LEGAL
                MATERIALS

> WEEK 3

MGT TEAM: SAME
EVENTS: SANDY ATL / CINDY W/FLU / MISSION BRIEF + RUN OF SHOW
NO GUEST LIST / DOSSIER / TIMING

INVITE LIST: WHO? WERE THEY THE RIGHT PEOPLE?
SALES: ORGANIZATIONAL DOCS DEVELOPMENT
EXTERNAL INPUT ON VA USE LATE FRI

FOUNDATION: ESTABLISHED
PRESSURE POINTS: MISSION BRIEF / LAST-MINUTE PREP /
HOW TO USE PARTNER EXPERTISE (LATE RESERVATIONS)

> MAY 6

PFA

UNDERSTANDING OF FACTS / PA IMPACT
DIDN'T FOLLOW SCRIPT
1ST BOARD MEETING

*Note: These are words captured in "short-hand", clearly under-standable both to all debrief participants as well as to the organization at-large, using a language the entire organization comprehends. This is critical for the Memorialization step; we need the entire organization to be able to benefit from the Debrief.

Of note, each line was written with approval from the full team. Nothing was pre-written, aside from what I captured in my own, personal notes. I solicited input, perspectives and observations from the full team, discussing each point verbally before committing it on the paper. In other words, I reconstructed this the same way as the "dogfighting" lines we saw previously.

Again, the "tape review" process can be facilitated by any existing data capture method available in any industry. Athletic coaches often have access to video recordings of what took place on the field or court; health care providers have data from their systems to determine how long, for example, it took from the placement of a prescription order to when the patient received medicine; sales teams track contact data, engagements made and kept, conversions and the like. The examples are countless, and the sources of data are plentiful. Indeed, almost every endeavor has some way of being able to capture what actually happened.

At the end of the day, taking the time to write what actually happened using short statements is well worth it. For one thing, the process helps fill in knowledge gaps for the leader, highlighting things he might have had no way of knowing.[82] Writing this data so that everyone in the room can see it, process it, analyze it, question it, and then maybe even add to it or otherwise use it—this is the fundamental point of the Reconstruction phase, and worth every minute. It's also critical that one person, specifically the Leader, is the person who writes what needs to be written. He or she is in the best position to summarize long statements, to synthesize multiple statements that all sort of say the same thing, to adjudicate which points are worthy of inclusion and which are points the team can talk about separately/later, and so on. This fact-gathering process requires advance thought, and the leader should consider—at the latest, the night prior—everything from how to capture and summarize the data, to how he intends to utilize the available space (a flip chart is only so big) to represent the history of events.

When I'm working on a project for a client, I organize my notes of what transpired each day and each week to help me quickly recall the sequence of events during the debrief. Yes, it can be easy to get side-tracked during Reconstruction, or to want to skip quickly to performance evaluation and Root Cause determination. It is essential that Leaders be ready to advise a team that wants to charge ahead, "Hang-on… we're not there yet!" It's critical that leaders be ready to take command, keep the focus on accuracy, and to hold team members accountable for applying the tenets of the Team Charter for team success.

> THEREFORE, WE START BY COMPARING THE RESULTS WE ACHIEVED WITH OUR STATED OBJECTIVES

Reconstruction Timing

Let's take a quick minute to address time expectations. The degree of urgency, coupled with the "seriousness" of the issues we have to address, will drive how much time we spend on the Reconstruction phase. The context of the debrief will have a critical effect on our timing as well. In a business setting, the Reconstruction phase is where we will likely spend the bulk of our time, roughly half of the overall time for our debrief, especially early on in the transition to a debrief-focused flow. Eventually, this process will go increasingly faster as the organization adopts time-saving techniques and the team becomes accustomed to the process. Just know that taking the time to reconstruct effectively is one of the main tenets of successful debriefs; *do not* skip or short-change this process. You'll truly be amazed at what you learn.

Step 2: Agree on the Fundamental Question(s) & Focus Points

In the RAPTOR debrief, we take the facts we collect in the Reconstruction phase and then determine which portions merit further exploration. We do this in a way that recognizes that our time together is precious and finite. Therefore, we start by comparing the results we achieved with our stated objectives. Phrased another way, the RAPTOR Debrief centers on whether or not we achieved our stated objectives. The point is to determine if we had any deltas or gaps, both good and bad. If we didn't achieve our Objectives, our analysis starts there; if we did achieve our objectives, we need to figure out if this was because of something we did correctly or because we had good luck. Either way, our Objectives will drive our initial focus, and then the context of the debrief will define what else it is we need to review. The basic process is exceedingly logical and, with a little critical thinking, the RAPTOR Debrief is very easy to execute. Unfortunately, not everyone who practices a form of debriefing uses this process. Let's take a quick moment to review a competing approach to better understand the value of the RAPTOR methodology.

An Example for Comparison: The Unstructured Debrief

A couple of years ago, I took part in a debrief led by a well-intentioned CEO whose purpose in calling us all together was exactly right—he wanted us to learn from our experience. We had just finished a product launch event, and the goal of the debrief was to determine—while the event was fresh in our minds—how we did and where we could improve in the future. We were fortunate that the event we had just hosted was fun, our team was in a good mood, it was a sunny day and our hotel was on the beach—giving us an exceedingly promising setup.

Unfortunately, the promise began to fade almost from the start. As a strong proponent of this debrief, I was shocked to learn that almost everyone who'd attended the conference was allowed to join. People who had only the loosest of affiliations with the organization were present; spouses and companions, as well as people who were strong supporters of our organization but who were not part of the core tactical planning team. Indeed, almost anyone who felt like spending some time debriefing was welcome and, to my absolute amazement—people came! This, of course, completely quelled our ability to tackle any difficult or controversial issues. Nobody on our core team was going to have those types of conversations in front of complete strangers, companions and "outsiders" in general, because the required psychological safety was absent.

We assembled in a big circle and the CEO started by saying something to the effect of, "I really just want to know what's on your mind on how we can improve for the next event. Let's go clockwise around the room and we'll just speak in sequence." With this as our structure—one similar to that used in other debriefs I've mentioned (effectively: "What went well?" "What didn't go well?")—and with a packed room gave everyone an immediate soapbox upon which to rant about whatever they wanted. As memory serves, we discussed the breakfast options at great length. We talked about all kinds of administrative points, from registration hiccups to speaker sequencing. We talked about a song one of the speakers played during her presentation (it turns out people really liked it). We talked about everything that anyone could think of, largely from the standpoint of criticism (except for the song), and without any focus. It was a full *three and a half hours* before we arrived at my place in the circle. By that point, I was more than a little frustrated, both with the process as a whole and with myself for letting it get to this point.

But instead of vocalizing my frustration I asked simply, "What was our objective this weekend?" The silence that followed showed the truth of the matter—no one knew the answer. I followed up with my summary of what I assumed we were trying to achieve (critically, we had never actually defined our objective for the weekend), and then my analysis of whether or not we had achieved it (I gave us a "pass" by stating it was "too early to tell"). My point was that our debrief should have been conducted <u>to determine whether or not the weekend was a success</u> and, if not, what steps we would need to take in order to ensure success at our product launch. As such, the breakfast options were irrelevant. The song was irrelevant. *MOST* of the things we talked about for three and a half hours were irrelevant, because they didn't answer the question of whether or not we had achieved our un-defined objectives. Our debrief was an absolute waste of time, despite being led with great intention, by very intelligent people who were truly looking to improve.

In hindsight, I hold myself fully accountable because I failed to speak up at the very beginning of the process. I should have saved us all a ton of heartache and wasted time by asking what our objectives were at the outset. I should have helped facilitate the debrief, starting out by making sure the right people attended. I failed my team that day and share this story with you in the hopes that you learn from my mistake.

The Effective Debrief Centers on Objectives

The take-away here is that our objectives should drive the debrief. If the objectives really matter (and they absolutely should), then they're our primary focus. Next in line are the coaching aspects we need to employ to improve team performance, which may or may not be intrinsic in our objectives. The nice thing about achievable, measurable objectives that are defined in time, is that it should be very easy to quantify whether or not we've achieved them. We simply ask "why" or "why not?" The formal title we'll use for this is developing the "Fundamental Question(s)" or FQ. Any additional items we want to review, based on the context of our debrief, we'll call "Focus Points" or FPs. Fundamental Questions are stated as questions. Focus Points are identified in whatever format makes the most sense; on a dogfighting mission I would circle these points on the board, for example.

Crafting the Fundamental Question

Let's return to our "dogfighting" example. If the Defensive Fighter was "gunned" ("shot down" by simulated bullets) by the Offensive Fighter, we would return to the objectives and do a quick comparison to determine our FQ. Remember, the Objectives for our "dogfighting" mission were to:

▶ *Defeat the Initial Attack*

▶ *Deny Subsequent Opportunities for the Offensive Fighter to Attack*

▶ *Escape from the fight, Neutralize the fight or Become the Offensive Fighter*

Where in time the Defensive Fighter was "gunned" drives which of these objectives we focus on—whether he was "gunned" during the initial attack or subsequent attacks affects how we address this specific lesson. Either way, our FQ would look something like this (where DF = Defensive Fighter and OF = Offensive Fighter):

* **WHY DIDN'T THE DF DEFEAT THE INITIAL ATTACK?**

OR

* **WHY DID WE ALLOW THE OF TO SUBSEQUENTLY AND SUCCESSFULLY ATTACK US?**

Either of these questions would be valid based on the actual end result, compared with our objectives. Most importantly, by framing our question in relation to our objectives, the debrief now has an active purpose. We know as a team what question we need to answer, and what outcome we should seek—a hypothesis we can test the next time we fly this mission regarding how to avoid today's poor outcome. Whether we choose to play games or follow a defined and repeatable methodology, we're positioned to come away with something valuable and worth noting. Framing the FQ in this manner is also a very simple process; we look at the objectives, determine what the gap was between actual and desired performance, and then ask WHY. "Why didn't we…?" or "Why did we…?"

Crafting Subsets of Fundamental Questions

Sometimes it becomes clear that we need to ask a couple of key questions, one a subset of the other, in order to maximize the debrief's effectiveness. In other words, by answering a particular question that may not even be directly tied to the objectives, we move towards the answer to our Fundamental Question. Going back to our dogfight example, we might ask something like this:

WHY DIDN'T THE DF DEFEAT THE INITIAL ATTACK?

WHY DIDN'T THE DF EXECUTE THE BRIEFED GAME PLAN?

In this case, our questioning demonstrates an advanced understanding of the facts. Asking the question this way suggests that something about the game plan and its execution likely answers the question about defeating the initial attack. Perhaps it was apparent during our tape review, and certainly it was obvious no later than the Reconstruction phase, that the Defensive Fighter didn't do what he was instructed to do in the mission briefing. That said, if the maneuver he attempted will likely drive the answer to our Fundamental Question, this question can be listed as a sub-set of the FQ. A common example I recall from the larger, more demanding missions I flew looks something like this:

WHY DIDN'T WE ACHIEVE BOMBS ON TARGET ON TIME (BOTOT)?

WHY WAS THE BOMBER "SHOT DOWN" EN ROUTE TO THE TARGET AREA?

Again, the two questions are clearly related. On a bombing mission, it is obvious that the bomber must survive to the target area. If the bomber is shot down and can't perform its mission, then the overall question can be answered by figuring out how to keep the bomber alive both to and through the target area. Ultimately, we understand that by answering the second question correctly, we most likely answer our Fundamental Question, and so we combine the two to efficiently achieve our results.

Armed with our FQ(s), we can now scan the Reconstruction for any other areas we need to focus on, based on the context of our debrief. Because we're always time-limited, which means we need to be efficient. Leaders must make a mental note of how much time they're spending *throughout* the debrief, to make sure they have enough time to cover the most important items for team improvement.

Focus Points

While a concentration on the Objectives drives how a leader will focus the debrief, context determines whether additional learning is needed to improve individual and team performance. This additional learning might be outside the bounds of what's covered while answering the Fundamental Question, but for very good reason. It could be that today's Focus Point would have been tomorrow's Fundamental Question, had we not addressed it today. Think back to the extremely-close pass I described in the "Pre-Brief." Had we not debriefed immediately, we may have hit one another on a subsequent engagement. A major consideration is how much time we choose to spend addressing a Focus Point in contrast to a Fundamental Question (usually, but not always, less time), the same basic concern outlined above. Here's what I've learned from fighter mission debriefs throughout my career:

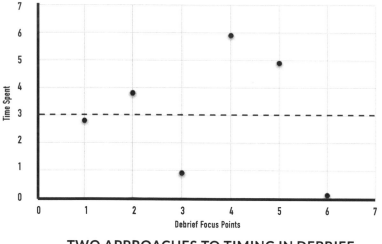

TWO APPROACHES TO TIMING IN DEBRIEF

When we treat each issue at the same level—that is, when we spend the same amount of time on each issue we highlight—*ALL* of the issues we're trying to address lose gravity—a point demonstrated by the dashed line on this chart. When, on the other hand, we treat each issue at an "appropriate" level (depicted by the dots), each one stands out accordingly. Teams pick up on this difference, and those who are in a position to witness the debrief unfold (the participants much more so than the leader), will absolutely appreciate this approach. In the same vein, they will absolutely NOT appreciate it when every issue is handled as though it carries the same level of weight.

In the end, how much time one assigns to the various issues in a debrief is a value judgment and is best done real-time and with help from the crowd. Here are my general rules of thumb for how I'll spend my time on items that aren't directly tied to the FQ:

▶ Is this an "Upgrade Ride"—a situation where we're training and evaluating an employee's ability to move to the next level? If the debrief is an Instructional debrief of an upgrade ride, I focus attention on areas that were previously listed as problems on previous grade sheets, as well as anything I noticed during execution that would likely be a potential problem area on a future mission.

▶ Is this a "Continuation Training" mission? And are there special emphasis items that need to be reviewed? If the debrief is of a Continuation Training mission, my focus is on answering our Fundamental Question, as well as anything else that stood out from a safety-of-flight or standards, tactics and checklists standpoint. If there are safety or execution highlights the squadron leadership wants emphasized, we'll also look at those points.

▶ Did something happen this go-around that could become a Fundamental Question next time? If so, this changes our approach. We might transition from a more laid-back approach to one where we acknowledge that while we were lucky today, we can't count on luck for success. We would make sure this won't happen the next time and extend the debrief accordingly.

▶ If the debrief is of a Combat mission or deployment, the focus is again on answering the question tied to the objectives, as well as anything tied to safety.

LEADERSHIP HIGHLIGHT

- The debrief leader is now in a position to help steer the initial vector of the conversation based on the context.

- Leaders should not abuse this privilege.

- This is another reason why we don't want outside facilitators coming in to lead our debriefs.

Remember that the focus is to determine how to gain as much knowledge as possible *on those subjects that really matter* in a reasonable amount of time. My counsel, especially when you first adopt the RAPTOR debrief in your organization, is to set aside enough time for this process so the focus can be on the mission, our achievement (or lack thereof) of the stated objectives, and how to improve our ability to meet or exceed our objectives next time. Free up your team's schedule and don't allow time to be the limiting factor. As time goes on, you'll learn how to do this extremely efficiently, and you'll also learn how to adapt the overall process to your organization's needs.

The Pizza Shop Example: A Quick Introduction

Let's end this section by reviewing the development of a Fundamental Question from the standpoint of a regular business, one that has nothing to do with fighter aviation. We'll look at the example of a pizza shop owner, one we'll touch on very briefly here and then carry through into the next chapter. We start with the following parameters:

OBJECTIVE: *100% on-time delivery of pizza*

RESULT: *25% of pizzas were delivered late*

We can see that the Fundamental Question jumps out—establishing the FQ is not typically a complicated process:

FUNDAMENTAL QUESTION:

WHY WERE WE ONLY 75% EFFECTIVE AT DELIVERING PIZZAS ON-TIME?

By starting with objectives and then evaluating our performance in relation to them, we quickly get to the point of the debrief. Like anything, this process takes some getting used to, but the debrief leader can accelerate learning by making sure *from the start* that the team as a whole agrees that the correct question has been identified. And since we know nothing else about this scenario yet, we can't determine whether there are any Focus Points. More on this in a bit.

Returning to the question of perspective: often, those not leading the debrief may well have a better grasp on what the FQ should be, primarily because they are under less pressure and enjoy more space to think. The leader should consider this, evaluate the input coming from a different perspective, and decide whether to incorporate that perspective into the discussion. In a RAPTOR Debrief, it's ultimately the leader's call on where the debrief will go. He takes his team's input and decides how to proceed. He's forced to make a judgment call, one of many, that will take place during the debrief; that's part of the job of being an Accountable Leader. Despite the challenge here, this ends up becoming one of the many benefits of this important approach: Leaders having the opportunity, and truly be called to *lead*.

STEP 3: Present the Driving Factors (Explore Possible Answers to the FQ)

Armed with our Fundamental Question(s) and Focus Points, we know the focus of our debrief. Now we shift to considering all *likely* answers—the Driving Factors (DFs)—to the questions we've posed, within reason. We decide how much the data we've collected during the Reconstruction can help us. I assure you that our Reconstruction highlights will not, however, magically hold all of the answers —and here is where critical thinking really comes into play.

There is a tendency in a debrief, and especially early on in our practice of debriefing, to gravitate towards obvious answers. When we're stressed and pressed for time, it's especially compelling to go with what jumps out at us first, and an answer that seems "good enough" is awfully enticing. Sometimes this "good enough" answer is the last thing that happened prior to the mistake in question. But the "last thing" is an insufficient answer, however, because it is rarely the true Root Cause of our problem. Sometimes this "good enough" answer presents itself as the "Group Think" answer. Someone suggests it, the crowd picks up on it, and it's easy to run with because everyone supports it. But what happens when you know in your gut it's not sufficient?

In order to get to the correct answer, we have to apply critical thinking. According to the Foundation for Critical Thinking, Critical thinking "is that mode of thinking—about any subject, content, or problem—in which the thinker improves the quality of his or her thinking by skillfully analyzing, assessing, and reconstructing it."[83] By applying critical thinking, we avoid the obvious mistake of looking at the last event prior to our issue, and identifying it as the answer to our question. Critical thinking compels us to gather as much data as possible before coming to any conclusions. To be sure, part of this data gathering took place during the Reconstruction, but not all. Believe it or not, we STILL don't have all of the details and the full perspectives we need to answer the Fundamental Question we just assigned. It took me a while to figure this out during my own development as a fighter pilot, as I'll illustrate here.

The Importance of Perspectives

The Air Force Weapons School is an extremely exclusive school. One of the ways the Weapons School F-15/F-22 squadron discerns who to admit is by providing prospective students with an "opportunity" to brief, lead and debrief a one vs. one mission—the "dogfight" I described earlier—with a current Weapons School instructor. This is a high-stakes, high-pressure mission that can make or break a prospective student's chances. We call these missions "look rides", and I remember my "look ride" vividly because of how much pressure I placed on myself to do well.

I spent the week prior solely focused on preparing and was incredibly nervous as the mission approached. The good news was that I was very comfortable briefing and I felt generally confident in my ability to fight a "dogfight" mission. That day, I'm happy to say, I had a really good day. On our last engagement, I was absolutely stunned when I was able to simulate using the F-15 gun to "shoot down" my Weapons School instructor in the first 30 seconds of the fight. Following this miraculous achievement, we were both out of gas and returned to base—I was beyond thrilled!

I led us through a debrief of our engagements, ending with the personal high note of my quick gun "kill." Once our debrief validated that I had, truly, achieved a valid gun "kill", I spent roughly 30 minutes "teaching" my opponent everything I could possibly think of to help him avoid the same result in the future. I was on top of the world, and a fly on the wall would have thought I did a pretty good job of teaching my "student" powerful ways to do better next time. The best part was that I felt my performance absolutely validated that I was qualified and ready to be accepted to the Weapons School!

Once I finished my debrief, I turned the room over to the real instructor of the day, and he outlined in broad strokes how I did. He told me my briefing was good, and that my in-flight leadership and execution was fine. He said that I had done a good job generally with the debrief and that he was going to focus his instruction on how I debriefed our last engagement. Inside I was brimming with pride, confident that the day was ending extremely well.

Then he began his analysis by advising me that I completely missed the mark.

I was floored. How could I have missed the mark on an engagement where I CLEARLY beat him, and quickly at that? How could I have missed the mark when I had given him so many outstanding techniques to help him avoid a similar result in the future? I was jarred awake from my reflections by his comments that went something like this:

Him: *With all of the great data you provided me, you never asked me the basic, core questions. Do you know what those questions are?*

Me: *Uhhh...I'm not sure?*

Him: *Let's start with the most fundamental question of all, namely 'What did you see?' Let's try it—[pointing at the point on the board where I was gunning him] 'At this point here where I'm maneuvering into a weapons solution against you, what did you see'?*

Me: *Hmmmm...*

Him: *If you had asked me what I saw at that point I would have told you that I saw a 'Master Caution' light, along with an 'Engine Fire' warning.*

Me: *(internally) Oh, no...*

Him: *If you had gone to the next fundamental step you would have asked me the second basic question, which is 'what did you want to do based on this information?' I would have told you that I figured I could try to troubleshoot the fire while still finishing up the engagement with you.*

Me: *(thinking) Oh boy...I can see where this is going...*

Him: *Then you would have come to the third basic question, which would have been 'what maneuver did you choose in order to troubleshoot while still engaging me?' I would have told you that I continued with my vertical jink [defensive maneuver] while spending most of my time looking at my engine instruments and not at you. I had no idea you were in a guns solution on me because I wasn't paying any attention to you.*

Me: (thinking) *Today just went from super-awesome to not-so-awesome in no time flat.*

Him: *Now, armed with this knowledge, how would you have adjusted your debrief?*

Me: (sheepishly) *I would have asked you why you didn't end the fight at the point where you saw the Master Caution and Engine Fire lights, recognizing that in training our priority is to not push the bounds of safety. The correct procedure would have been for you to call 'Knock-it-Off' [end the fight], me pointing our formation back towards the base, me giving you the lead and backing you up as we run the 'Engine Fire in Flight' checklist.*

Him: *Good call. In fact, the debrief would have had a completely different emphasis from the one you led if it had been done correctly. Most importantly, the conclusions we reached would have been just as dramatically different. As a bonus, we also would have saved about 25 minutes of our lives that we'll never get back by having focused on the real problem, which was my decision to continue fighting while I was dealing with a potential engine fire. THAT, my friend, is what I want you to remember from today's mission.*

Now remember, the Reconstruction I led was just fine—we had captured all of the correct information we needed to properly address our fight. My knowledge of the procedures was not at fault as I was well-primed to lead us through a quality debrief. The mistake I made was not probing enough, not gathering additional facts by way of eliciting the full perspective of what was happening in my opponent's cockpit. By not exploring my opponent's perspective of the issue in question I instinctively selected Driving Factors that made sense to me, were perfectly logical, answered the Fundamental Question brilliantly…and were all technically incorrect. I failed to elicit the ONLY Driving Factor that mattered in this case and spoiled the debrief in the process. Because my instructor was trying to advance my understanding of the methodology in play, he wasn't going to volunteer anything; he was going to make me work for data. I can promise you the quality of my debriefs went up exponentially thereafter, and I've clearly NEVER forgotten this fundamental lesson.

A quick exploration of this series of questions is boiled down to the following:

▶ "What did you see?": An exploration of our teammates' perspective. This is where we seek to understand a perspective of the events from the standpoint of someone other than us. It's a vital step in the debrief process, and one that we need to become accustomed to regularly asking of all our teammates.

▶ "What did you want to do?": An exploration of the decision-making process of our teammate. As author and poker player Annie Duke suggests, "What makes a decision great is not that it has a great outcome. A great decision is the result of a good process, and that process must include an attempt to accurately represent our own state of knowledge."[84]

▶ "How did you go about doing it?": Allows for an analysis of the execution that stems from the decision that was made. Here we get into the technique and methodology, whereas the previous question gets to the core understanding and decision-making involved in a question.

The bottom line is that if we don't approach the debrief armed with this body of knowledge, ready to ask these questions, we can absolutely miss the point of the debrief. This wastes time and generates the wrong conclusions—even if we're working really hard and doing our best. *Most importantly, understanding the various team members' perspectives allows us to lead them better, because we understand how they see the world.* There is no better source of leadership wisdom than the perspective of a follower by way of the debrief, plain and simple.

LEADERSHIP HIGHLIGHT

- This is where PERSPECTIVES become SO CRITICAL to success.
- With every separate individual involved in a process comes a separate, and often fundamentally different, perspective.
- We need to ask the critical questions before launching into a determination: What did you see? What did you want to do? How did you go about doing it?

Driving Factors and Focus Areas Guides

Armed with the knowledge of how important perspectives are, let's now look at sources of our answers to our FQs and Focus Points. One of the major areas to explore will always be the plan itself. And, given that the leader is ultimately responsible for the plan, he needs to be able to begin the process by looking inward to determine whether his approach, leadership, planning or other action (or lack of action) drove the results we're examining. It may well be that someone on the team didn't do what they were supposed to do, or didn't do their part well enough. That's fine, and is something that can be coached to. But if what they were tasked to do wasn't the right thing to begin with, their mistake is completely overshadowed. The leader holds full responsibility for the plan, its quality and its appropriateness. As such, the leader must be prepared to share responsibility for any negative outcomes resulting from the plan itself. This is the approach that moves us into the realm of "Level-3" debriefs, and Jim Collins' Level 5 leadership. The only honest way to get here is for the leader to lead their own debriefs, and for leaders to openly recognize their faults—IN FRONT OF THEIR SUBORDINATES.

What follows are a few suggestions to assist in the answer-development process, with recommendations for both Level 2 and Level 3 debriefs:

LEVEL 2 ANALYSIS DRIVING FACTORS / FOCUS AREAS

PLAN ADHERENCE	PROCESS	TEAM
Did we follow the plan?	Did we follow our established process?	Did every member of the team contribute as expected?
Did we accomplish/ achieve the desired number of events/ contacts/things?	Did we abide by our standards/check-lists/tactics?	Did every team-member achieve their part of the plan?
Did we achieve them on time?	Did we adhere to our training and repli-cate the established system?	Did the team mem-bers support each other?
Did we accomplish/ achieve them within the budget?	Was there an op-portunity to deviate from the established process to benefit the team?	Did the plan support team development or promote individu-alism?

PLAN ADHERENCE	PROCESS	TEAM
Was there an opportunity to deviate from the plan in a positive way?	Does the process allow for judgement calls when it comes to process deviations? If not, should it?	Did awards/ competition/ standards of performance (or lack thereof) help or hinder execution?
Did the plan allow for independent decision-making?		Do the members of the team have the necessary skills to succeed?
		Are the members of the team making the right decisions?

LEVEL 3 ANALYSIS DRIVING FACTORS / FOCUS AREAS

GUIDANCE	COMMUNICATION	TEAM
Was the plan the right one?	Did I communicate the plan correctly/ in sufficient detail to enable success?	Was my leadership supportive to my team?
Was it sufficient to address the needs throughout?	Did I communicate on a frequency and with a language my team uses and understands?	Did I establish the correct culture to enable successful teamwork?
Did the plan include enough detail to address all the challenges?	Did I verify comprehension of my team members?	Was I inclusive in the planning process?
Did the plan sufficiently address contingencies?	Did I solicit team member input to improve understanding/improve the plan?	Did I provide the real-time guidance necessary to meet the OBJECTIVE(S)?

GUIDANCE	COMMUNICATION	TEAM
Was the plan executable based on the skills and expertise of the team?	Did/could team members provide active feedback during execution so leadership might deviate as necessary?	Did I make myself available to adjust the plan to changing circumstances?
		Was I responsive to my team during all phases of plan execution?
		Have I empowered my team to make independent decisions that support achievement of our OBJECTIVE(S)?

One of the keys to success in this phase of the debrief is that the leader captures the possible Driving Factors on the board for all to see. This will be especially useful when it comes to Root Cause determination, as either the Root Cause itself, or critical elements that help in determining the Root Cause, will stand out if the Driving Factors are on the board. In all cases, the team needs to critically analyze the selected Driving Factors to determine the reason for the gap between actual performance and stated objectives, both good and bad.

STEP 4: Thoroughly Agree on the Root Cause(s)

Root Cause determination is another opportunity for the leader to lead courageously. Armed with the facts, the proposed answers to our Fundamental Question, and our analysis of the various perspectives of why what happened did, we can arrive at a solid answer that meets our minimum standards. Here's where we really make our money as leaders because—assuming we've selected the correct Fundamental Question and Driving Factors—we're going to soon pinpoint exactly where we went wrong, if we failed to meet our objectives. We must apply the lessons of my Weapons School "look ride" to do this correctly. I propose the following two key questions to help guide this process:

▶ Does our selected Root Cause *honestly* answer the question we asked?

▶   If so, does it answer our question *sufficiently*?

The Level-1 standard of sufficiency says that if we have an answer, almost any answer, we've done our job. This is DANGEROUS. False Root Cause identification drives "false learning"; we can ruin our organizations by training our teams to do things the wrong way, by implementing the wrong "fixes" and by allowing our teams to believe that we're on the right track when we are not.

The Level-2 standard of sufficiency says that if we identify an area—potentially THE area—where our performance started to fall apart, we've done our job. Here we arrive at answers like, "The reason why ship two sank is that ship one turned into and hit ship two." This is a fact and seems pretty obvious. It answers the question, to some degree. But the answer is insufficient. WHY did the ship turn into the other one? WHO is responsible for the decision that led to the outcome? WHO might have prevented this mistake, and WHY didn't they? WHO had the critical information at the time decisions were made, and did they share that information appropriately? These are some of the questions that really matter.

"5 Whys"

One method for getting to the Root Cause is to ask the question "Why" until you stop getting useful responses. The technique is known as the "5 Why's" and traces its roots to Sakichi Toyota. According to the website "mindtools.com," this technique "is most effective when the answers come from people who have hands-on experience of the process being examined. It is remarkably simple: when a problem occurs, you drill down to its root cause by asking "why?" five times. Then, when a counter-measure becomes apparent, you follow it through to prevent the issue from recurring." Furthermore, this methodology is highlighted as being useful "for troubleshooting, quality improvement and problem solving, but it is most effective when used to resolve simple or moderately difficult problems."[85]

George Koenigsaecker talks about this process in his book, Leading the Lean Enterprise Transformation. He offers, "From personal experience, I suggest that about 90 percent of all quality problems can be solved just by getting the work group together, at the exact time of the quality incident, and then asking why five times. (After the work team asks why five times, you will have found a root cause solution for 90 percent of daily quality issues. The next 10 percent of quality problems get progressively harder to solve.)"[86]

The point of this process is to again avoid jumping to the conclusion that the last thing to happen before our highlighted question is the Root Cause. Drilling down into a subject as deep as the team can go helps ensure the process is clean. That said, it takes effort to follow through with this kind of analysis. Says Koenigsaecker, "As simple and powerful as this is, most people almost never do it...This makes for an interesting cultural dilemma: We have, by far, the most efficient quality problem-solving tool and the easiest to learn, but it is very difficult to get people to practice it."[87] Thus it is that the leader has the mandate to apply this approach, and to do so correctly, to ensure the results are valid.

"Appreciation"

Another approach to Root Cause analysis is called "Appreciation". This approach was developed by the U.S. military and was designed to help commanders understand facts, problems or situations in battle. Returning to mindtools.com, "Using Appreciation is easy. Starting with a fact, you first ask the question "So what?" – in other words, what are the implications of that fact? Why is this fact important? You then continue asking that question until you have drawn all possible conclusions from it."[88] We'll explore an example of Appreciation applied in the next chapter under the section titled, *Mr. Smith's (Former Equifax CEO's) Testimony to Congress.*

The idea behind both techniques is to not be satisfied with the first answer that springs to mind, but to keep digging. Ultimately, by continuing to ask the key, probing questions, the quality of the answers improves to the point where the answer is deemed sufficient to be labeled as the source of the problem.

Ishikawa or Fishbone Diagram

The Fishbone Diagram is described as such because the effect or issue under analysis is shown at the end of a series of lines that look much like a fish skeleton:

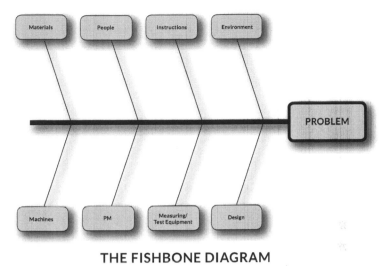

THE FISHBONE DIAGRAM

Structure as outlined at http://www.au.af.mil/au/awc/awcgate/nasa/root_cause_analysis.pdf

The lines are so drawn because the structure of the tool is designed to help identify a range of causes that ultimately lead to the Root Cause.

The website pmstudycircle.com offers the following overview of the approach: "The fishbone diagram uses a brainstorming technique to collect the causes and come up with a kind of mind map which shows you all identified causes graphically. Sometimes it happens that the most obvious cause turns out to be minor and the cause thought to be a minor one was causing the issue. This diagram gives you an opportunity to think more thoroughly about the root cause of the problem, which leads to a robust resolution. The fishbone diagram forces you to consider all possible causes of a problem instead of focusing on the most obvious one. Here causes are grouped into several categories to easily identify the correct source of the variation."[89]

Your team can capture potential causes of whatever problem you're exploring based on the industry at play. The fundamental approach is one that is both intuitive and powerful. As long as the team is clear on the methodology and the leader is versed in how to lead the brainstorming session, the Fishbone Diagram approach can be an outstanding tool to arrive at the correct Root Cause of a given problem.

Taking Accountability to the Next Level

The Level-3 standard of sufficiency for leaders always returns to the questions, "How could I have planned better, briefed better, led better? Ultimately, how could I have done a better job of setting conditions for my team's success so that they could have won, or won bigger and better?" With the privilege and associated perks of leadership comes the FULL responsibility for the decisions made.

Let's further explore Level-3 sufficiency, especially when it comes to the issue of responsibility. When I was a cadet at the Air Force Academy, I awoke one day to the horrific story of the accidental shoot-down of two U.S. Blackhawk helicopters by two U.S. Air Force F-15Cs. Everyone aboard the helicopters was killed; 26 lives were lost as a result of a series of mistakes. The Air Force charged one officer, the controller responsible for airspace control at the time, with dereliction of duty. One of the F-15 pilots was charged with negligent homicide and dereliction of duty, as were four other members of the controlling crew aboard the Airborne Warning and Control

System (AWACS). The captain was eventually acquitted of the charges and, following an investigation, the charges against the others were dropped.[90]

The Chief of Staff of the Air Force at the time, General Ron Fogleman, declared that he was satisfied with the results of the court proceedings and investigations. Specifically, he noted:

> *"...the outcome was appropriate and just; no one was court-martialed who should not have been, or vice-versa, or issued letters of reprimand, Article 15s, and so forth. But I was appalled...when I asked the question, 'let me see the evaluation reports on the people.' I discovered that none of what they had done was in those reports."* [91]

General Fogleman went on to personally issue "letters of evaluation describing their failure that became a permanent part of each individual's record. For the two F-15 pilots, three officers on the AWACS aircraft, and two generals in the chain of command, this action effectively ended their careers in the Air Force. General Fogleman also grounded the pilots and AWACS crew members, and disqualified them from duties in flying operations for three years." [92]

The point here is that leadership means bearing tremendous responsibility. I would argue that it is common for outgoing military commanders who have successfully completed their command tours to breathe a huge sigh of relief after the change-of-command ceremony. I've seen it in person and felt it myself. The fact of the matter is that commanders carry a burden with them everywhere they go, one that lasts until the command tour is complete.

That said, the more willing you are as a leader to accept blame for failure—legitimate acceptance, not forced, coerced or pretend—the more likely your team is going to be to respect you. This humble and accepting approach sets the conditions for psychological safety. I repeat—this effort cannot be fake. Your team will see through any insincerity immediately, thereby ruining your credibility as a leader. Owning your faults and assigning personal blame for areas where you could and should have done better is truly the mark of an accountable leader. That's what we're really looking for in accountable leadership.

At the same time, you must always give credit for success to your team. They're the ones doing the heavy lifting, they're the ones in the trenches. They're the ones you depend on to get the job done, and the ones who have ultimately done it. I witnessed this in the hospital I volunteer at: a nurse leader was publicly lauded for having achieved a critical and difficult benchmark in patient safety. Without ANY hesitation, she immediately deflected the recognition to her team, lauding their perseverance and highlighting how awesome it was to see them celebrate their success. That nurse understands Accountable Leadership, and is a personal role model for me!

LEADERSHIP HIGHLIGHT

As a leader, you bear the responsibility for the decisions that are made at every level of the company. As such, you're likely going to be the person who did make the mistake, which is all the more reason why you should take responsibility publicly.

A Way of Thinking About Root Cause Establishment

Functionally speaking, assigning the Root Cause is on-par with making a case in a court of law. I've personally practiced this process as if I were presenting a case to a jury of my peers; the decision I'm about to make as to the Root Cause(s) of our experience has to be convincing to "the jury." If it isn't, I'm probably wrong in my assessment. This approach forces the leader to think critically, go beyond the obvious, and to really seek the truth. Only when the entire team agrees that they have the correct result can the leader rest.

The leader must strive to get at least a *majority* of people to agree on the Root Cause. I'm not arguing for 100% buy-in, as there will often be detractors who aren't yet at a level (experience, process understanding or otherwise) where they can appreciate the conclusion. There may also be times where the Root Cause hurts a bit, and those who are hurt don't appreciate it. This is all part of growth and team development.

Again, this approach is centered on honesty and truth, two values that cannot be compromised in this process.

Quantifying Root Causes—Sharing Responsibility

I will also say that where judgment and subjectivity come into play, there can be differing views of what caused the issue. This is OK and doesn't need to interrupt the process. The discussion leading up to Root Cause establishment is probably the most valuable part of the process. This is also where leaders have the flexibility to assign differing levels of responsibility, to suggest or decide which of the Root Causes is the most important. It's perfectly acceptable to say that 50% of the Root Cause is due to X and the other 50% to Y. It's also perfectly acceptable to say that 20% is due to Nancy's error and 80% due to poor leadership. This isn't an exact science, nor will anyone ever ask for mathematical proof. The numbers say that blame is being shared, and that a couple of different factors led to the result. What is important is that everyone can see on the board in front of them what the Root Cause(s) is or are, and how much weight the leader assigns to each.

STEP 5: Organize a Plan to Improve or to Maintain Success

Once we've assigned the Root Cause we must then either 1) Develop the appropriate "Fix" in the case of poor performance, or 2) Determine the way-ahead in the event we met or exceeded our objectives (how are we going to replicate our good performance?). ***This is the whole point of the RAPTOR Debrief.*** I firmly believe that the debrief process serves NO PURPOSE if our team walks out of the room without a clear understanding of how we're going to proceed.

I've been leading incredibly focused debriefs for over two decades now—and I've developed a few pet peeves in the process. One of these is hearing people say, "We learned a lot of important lessons today!" My question is always, "Really? What is your *proof* that you've learned something?" In my experience, unless we change a plan, a policy or a procedure, I firmly contend we haven't learned anything. In fact, we're bound to go forward *making the exact same mistake the next time around…* because we haven't changed a thing. The only way to demonstrate learning is by making active changes to the way we think and behave.

Determining the Fix is the process of making these active changes, of arming ourselves with the game plan for how we can improve our performance, even if things went well. And because we're going to define the "correct" way to move out next time, we have to take the time to craft this step appropriately.

How We Address Poor Outcomes

If our execution was poor, and if things didn't go as well as planned, we either emphasize how we should have properly executed the plan as it was crafted (human error), how we should have made better decisions (human error), or how we will develop and implement the required change(s) to our plan, policy or procedure (process error). In all cases, the fundamental point is to capture IN WRITING how we're going to make a change to improve. We do this both to reinforce our conclusions (there's something powerful about capturing information in writing), as well as to have these conclusions readily available for future planning. We want to be able to reference our growing library of debrief conclusions to avoid repeating mistakes *across our entire organization* in the future. Key Point: As noted in the previous chapter, if our outcome was positive—if we achieved our objectives—but it wasn't because of our good work, we treat this almost as if the outcome was negative, at least from a process standpoint. Winning through luck, or because our opponents had a bad day, is not the way we want to win.

Before we go through the process of "Fix" determination, however, let's think about this concept a little deeper. A "Fix" is what we believe will correct behavior or adjust performance and drive better results. But because we don't have proof of those improved results until we actually implement our "Fix," our "Fix" is really just a hypothesis. Please don't get me wrong—the "Fix" is probably the best mental model we have to address our need, but *until we act on it—until we've tested our theorem—we really haven't learned anything.*

That said, we should be collaborating with our team members in every scenario to determine what needs to change to prevent a recurrence of the problem. The one partial exception is when the problem lies with the leader and his performance. It's only partial because the leader needs to lead with his or her best recommendation on what needs to happen, but still remain subject to the collective wisdom of the team to make certain his recommendation makes sense.

"The Fix" has to be something with teeth. It can be anything from the implementation of a correct procedure that wasn't followed, to a change in plans, policies, or procedures that will likely enable future success. A generic statement like "we're going to do better" or "we'll win next time" is NOT a fix, but rather a meaningless platitude. "The Fix" is ultimately that thing which, had it been done at the time of execution, would have prevented our mistake. We'll look at an example of what this looks like in the next chapter.

How We Address Positive Outcomes

One of the trials we face as leaders is dealing with success. This may sound odd, but it's a fact. Achieving success carries with it the responsibility for positioning the organization to be able to replicate it. Hitting the mark once, and then failing to repeat, offers only temporary joy; the expectation for a winning organization is that it continues to win. Any quality organization faces this challenge; it's why it's almost easier for a new leader to come into a failing organization. Expectations are low, and the leader has a lot of room to win by achieving ever-increasing levels of success.

A properly applied debrief allows a team to quickly determine the Root Cause of why it achieved success, so that the team can then determine how to *maintain* its success. If the team determines that their success is due to good luck or co-operative competitors, we follow the process outlined in the previous segment. It the team determines that its success was legitimate, if it properly determines a Root Cause, then the team can determine what it will take to continue to win. Codifying what the necessary steps are to achieve this, and capturing these steps in a way that the team understands what to do are key to future success. The answer must be just as clear as in the case of mission failure; there should be no question in the minds of the team members what it will take to keep winning.

Finishing with the Fix

We conclude our Fix determination process by confirming agreement with the rest of the team. This isn't always about getting their buy-in as much as it is about ensuring comprehension. If we're talking about an "upgrade" scenario, where we're teaching a new member of our tribe how "we" do things, it's especially important that the "student" understands why you're coming to the conclusions you're reaching.

The litmus test I always used when I was leading flying debriefs was to ask myself, "If we had done what we now propose as The Fix while airborne, would we have achieved our desired result?" If I could reasonably and honestly answer "yes" then I was comfortable with our Fix. If not, we would keep analyzing until I reached the level of comfort necessary to continue. The exact same technique applies in business.

In all cases, we end with a statement to the effect of: "If

we had done X in this way, we would have achieved our objectives." Everyone on the team should see it, feel it, and believe it for the process to have worked.

STEP 6: Rapidly Improve by "Memorialization"

Arguably the second-most important part of this process is documenting the findings and conclusions of the debrief. Documenting our outcomes allows us to file them away somewhere accessible, enabling us to review them prior to planning our next mission. This was a particularly useful technique I learned way back when I was originally qualifying on the F-15. At the squadron, we kept a binder with a record of the previous missions' outcomes—notes taken by students and instructors on what to expect on certain missions. This binder was incredibly useful, because it helped new students avoid repeating the mistakes of those who had gone before. In the process, it helped advance my understanding of what I was about to do immeasurably. I learned so much just trying to not make someone else's mistakes, rapidly accelerating my learning and helping me perform better. This process developed into the habit of referring to my notes from previous missions as part of my preparation for the next day's flight.

Part of what drives the necessity of this approach is that life is going increasingly quickly. If we don't sit down and focus, really focus on what we need to do to achieve success, it is highly likely we'll have a hard time doing so. We're pulled in so many different directions, and it's a fundamentally bad assumption that we're going to be able to "pull it all together" and execute well without really thinking through our plan in advance. We flew so many different types of missions during my days as a fighter pilot that unless we sat down and truly focused on the mission we were flying next, we ran the risk of underperforming. And nobody likes to under-perform.

> " IF WE DIDN'T SUCCEED TODAY, FOCUS ON HOW CLOSE WE WERE TO ACHIEVING SUCCESS. FIND A WAY TO MOTIVATE THE TEAM TO DO BETTER NEXT TIME, EVEN IN THE FACE OF A HORRIBLE DEFEAT

I saw several different versions of debrief memorialization, some better than others from the standpoint of pure learning. My favorite is the student binder version that I described from my early F-15 days. I also found that the F-16 Weapons School community practiced this process exceedingly well: they made their students write a one-page summary of the results of every debrief. They added these summaries to a master binder that anyone could refer to in support of their mission planning efforts. The key is that *everyone* had access to this data for mission planning, meaning that *everyone* stood to benefit from the learning of *any* individual pilot. This was a best-practice, and something I offer to companies and organizations everywhere.

Clearly, if there are any "to-do's" that stem from the debrief, it's essential that someone be assigned the responsibility to follow-up and ensure completion. Few things are more personally frustrating coming out of a debrief than everyone shaking hands, smiling, and doing NOTHING about anything that was just decided. It's critical that someone take on the responsibility for "closing the loop" on any open tasks.

CONCLUSION

And that's...*almost* it. We've now learned the RAPTOR Debrief in a nutshell, but now comes the time when we have to apply one of the lessons identified earlier: be positive! If we didn't succeed today, focus on how close we were to achieving success. Find a way to motivate the team to do better next time, even in the face of a horrible defeat. And when we do succeed, *celebrate the victories*! Highlight team and individual successes. Make the Debrief a process the team looks forward to repeating in the future. This isn't easy, and it goes against the grain in many cases, but it can have a game-changing effect on your organization.

Otherwise, the RAPTOR Debrief is a very simple framework—one that's even easier to accomplish once you've started internalizing and practicing it. I recommend starting with simple, everyday issues. Debrief those to a level of sufficiency and then move on to bigger, more challenging problems. Then, when you're comfortable with the process, bring the debrief into your company or organization and start changing your organizational DNA. And then make sure to watch as your teams start to gel, and you start to produce consistently better performance! This is the whole point.

SUMMARY

STEP 1: RECONSTRUCT WHAT HAPPENED

▶ Reconstruction examples.

▶ Reconstruction done correctly is a visual capture of the truth.

▶ The timing of a reconstruction.

STEP 2: AGREE ON THE FUNDAMENTAL QUESTION(S) AND FOCUS POINT(S)

▶ An example of the unstructured debrief.

▶ Everything debrief-wise centers on the objectives.

▶ How to craft a Fundamental Question.

▶ Crafting subsets of the Fundamental Question.

▶ How to develop Focus Points.

▶ The pizza shop example.

STEP 3: PRESENT THE DRIVING FACTORS (EXPLORING THE POSSIBLE ANSWERS)

- ▶ The importance of perspectives.

- ▶ Guides for developing Driving Factors and Focus Areas.

STEP 4: THOROUGHLY AGREE ON THE ROOT CAUSE

- ▶ A way of thinking about Root Cause establishment.

- ▶ How to quantify Root Causes.

STEP 5: ORGANIZE A PLAN TO IMPROVE OR MAINTAIN SUCCESS

- ▶ How to address poor outcomes.

- ▶ How to address positive outcomes.

- ▶ Finishing with the Fix.

STEP 6: RAPIDLY IMPROVE BY MEMORIALIZATION

- ▶ Always end on a positive note!

CHAPTER 7

AN EXAMPLE AND TWO FOCUSED CASE STUDIES

SAY WHAT YOU MEAN. MEAN WHAT
YOU SAY. DON'T SAY IT MEAN.

John Helion

A rmed with this tool we call the RAPTOR Debrief and given that you most likely aren't flying high-performance fighter aircraft, let's look at a practical application in the business world. We'll return to our example of the "Pizza Shop", a restaurant that recently experienced a day where they under-performed by only delivering 75% of their pizzas on time. The context of this debrief is along the lines of a "Continuation Training" mission in that there is no "upgrade training" taking place. This is a regular day in the office, and the results simply aren't as good as expected, based on the set objectives. We'll take this debrief from the point where everyone has done their "tape review", the leader has asked for any alibis, and he's now focused on following the process appropriately. He begins by reminding everyone of the objective, a subset of his Intent or End State, where his pizza joint is the most reliable pizza restaurant in town for on-time deliveries:

OBJECTIVE: *100% on-time delivery of pizza*

Next, he does a re-cap of the plan with his team, the outlines of which are as follows:

▶ The plan for the evening called for lower manning than usual based on historical data that showed that when there was heavy rainfall in the area, pizza deliveries for this shop oddly went *down*, not up. As such, the owner only scheduled one delivery person for the whole evening;

▶ Because of the anticipated volume, the owner set this particular day as a payroll and quarterly tax return day, anticipating that the two cooks, the register clerk and delivery person were likely sufficient for the day.

STEP 1: Reconstruct what happened.

Once the leader has reminded everyone of the basic outline of the plan, he then leads the Reconstruction of what took place. In this Reconstruction, the leader, in conjunction with his team, will have noted the following:

* *THE STORE EXPERIENCED LOWER-THAN-USUAL CALL VOLUME THAT DAY;*

* *THE PRIMARY DELIVERY PERSON SHOWED UP TO WORK TWO HOURS LATE;*

* *THE TEAM WAS LATE DELIVERING PIZZAS ON 25% OF THEIR DELIVERIES;*

* *HEAVY RAIN CAUSED MAJOR TRAFFIC DELAYS THROUGHOUT THE CITY THROUGHOUT THE DAY;*

* *THE OWNER SPENT A LOT OF THE AFTERNOON WORKING ON PAYROLL AND QUARTERLY TAXES;*

* *THE SHOP EXPERIENCED A 55-MINUTE POWER OUTAGE THAT STARTED AT 3:30 PM;*

* *THE STORE RAN OUT OF PEPPERONI HALFWAY THROUGH THE EVENING AND THE OWNER HAD TO RUN TO THE GROCERY STORE TO SECURE MORE.*

STEP 2: Agree on the Fundamental Question(s) and Focus Point(s).

It's clear upon looking at the Reconstruction and comparing the results with the objective that several of the reconstruction statements highlight the one glaring issue: the team was late delivering pizzas 25% of the time. Since the objective was to be 100% on-time with all deliveries, the Fundamental Question stands out clearly:

OBJECTIVE: *100% on-time delivery of pizza.*

RESULT: *25% of pizzas were delivered late.*

FUNDAMENTAL QUESTION:

WHY WERE WE ONLY 75% EFFECTIVE AT DELIVERING PIZZAS ON-TIME ?

If we surmise from the start that the reason we failed to deliver the pizzas was that the delivery person failed to show up on time, we might build in a sub-FQ:

WHY WERE WE ONLY 75% EFFECTIVE AT DELIVERING ON-TIME PIZZAS?

WHY DID THE DELIVERY PERSON SHOW UP TWO HOURS LATE?

STEP 3: Present the Driving Factors.

At first glance, several of the assembled facts might be appropriate answers to our Fundamental Question. This is where an understanding of the original plan is important, and why we lead off our Debrief with this information. Knowing the plan and comparing it to actual execution helps us understand where the real answers lie. In addition, we know what Standards, Tactics and Checklist items the team follows. When it comes to the Standards, the expectation is that everyone shows up to work at the scheduled time. In terms of Tactics, nothing stands out; but as we'll see, there's probably room for growth in terms of the Checklists.

As we go through the process of determining our Driving Factors, the leader needs to talk through the facts, in an effort to gather critical perspectives along the way. The key is to avoid jumping to conclusions, and to be open to a variety of possibilities that help answer the question we've identified. In the course of drawing up his Driving Factors, the leader either publicly shares, or internally determines, the following:

▶ The owner clearly did not expect the delivery person to show up two hours late, and herein lies a potential answer to the Fundamental Question. This should be one of our Driving Factors;

▶ During execution, and based on the fact that the delivery person showed up late, one of the cooks ended up doing deliveries and the pizza-making process slowed down substantially. This also factors in on the deliberations, though this point itself isn't a clear Driving Factor. This seems to rather be a mitigating factor;

▶ It also turns out that the cooks, given the lower-than-usual call volume, spent some of their free time messing around with some of the gadgets they didn't often use. This ultimately led to a blown fuse and a 55-minute search for the fix. Here's another potential answer to our Fundamental Question, one that should be added to our list of Driving Factors;

▶ Finally, when the store ran out of pepperoni the owner was informed immediately. He secured "emergency" supplies in less than 15 minutes, and there were no pepperoni pizza orders during this time. Even though this point initially seems like a "juicy" potential answer, it turns out it's not a Driving Factor, although it might be a Focus Point.

Therefore, based on what we've just explored, our Driving Factors include:

* **THE DELIVERY PERSON SHOWED UP TWO HOURS LATE TO WORK;**

* **THE COOKS BLEW A FUSE, LEADING TO A LOSS OF POWER FOR 55 MINUTES.**

It's important that we not get confused or lose focus when confronted with all the facts captured during the reconstruction.

We have to critically analyze all of the available information to find only those items that potentially answer our FQ. Once we have our Driving Factors, it's time to further analyze these to determine the "Root Cause" of our failure to meet our objectives.

The leader should begin his analysis by talking to the delivery person and asking for his perspective. Again, this conversation presumes the necessary degree of psychological safety for the subject to speak the truth. The leader needs honest, sincere feedback—he will only be able to get to the truth of the matter if the employee *trusts* that the process is <u>not about finding fault for the sake of blame, but is rather about figuring out how to do better in the future!</u> Taking from the example of my Weapons School "look ride" debrief, the leader needs to understand what the employee "saw," "thought," or "understood" about the events before trying to determine Root Cause. In this case, the leader would likely begin by asking the delivery person—whom we'll call Tom, for the sake of this illustration—about his awareness was of the schedule for that day. The dialogue might go something like this:

Leader: *So, Tom, tell me—what time did you think you needed to be at work?*

Tom: *Honestly, I expected to start work that day at 6 PM.*

Leader: *Why did you think you needed to be there at 6 PM instead of 4 PM? We typically start our evening shift at 4 PM. [The first "Why" in the process]*

Tom: *Well, ummm...well frankly because when you set the schedule two weeks ago, you mentioned that, due to the low expected volume and the fact that your son was going to be in town from college and was going to work a few hours that day, you didn't need me until 6 PM.*

Leader: *[inwardly] 'Oh, fudge...I completely forgot...my son had to cancel his trip home and I forgot to change the schedule...' [outwardly] Great point! Thank you for reminding me!*

STEP 4: Thoroughly agree on the Root Cause(s).

Already, we're starting to get to the crux of the issue: a preventable scheduling snafu that was uncovered BEFORE Tom was blamed. Taking into account that Tom has a perception of the events that may be more accurate than the leader's, the leader takes the time to ask the basic series of "Perception" questions: what did you see/think/believe? What was your plan based on what you saw/thought/believed? How did you go about executing your plan? In this example, asking the perception question saved the day and gave the leader an opportunity to avoid a line of thought that would have taken him down a very wrong path.

Let's consider this question in terms of the 5 Whys paradigm, mapping the thought process the leader has followed in his head, which needs to be shared with the rest of his team so everyone understands:

▶ Why did the delivery person show up at 6 PM instead of 4 PM? *Because that's the time he was scheduled to arrive as per the master schedule.*

▶ Why did the schedule say to show up at 6 PM? *Because the leader planned on his son working until 6 PM. When his son's schedule changed, he failed to update the calendar.*

▶ Why did the leader fail to update the calendar? *Because once he sets the calendar he doesn't regularly review it for accuracy. His process is to set it and effectively forget it.*

▶ Why doesn't the leader have a better process for updating the calendar? *Probably because he's never had an issue with this system. The system had not yet been tested.*

In this case, it only takes us 3-4 Whys to get to the root of the issue (arguably, the fact that the process failed was established on the 3rd Why), which is perfectly fine. Sometimes it might take more than five to get to the Root Cause. Either way, we've established the Root Cause. Another interesting take-away is that if we left it with only a Level 2 Analysis, we'd find our selves in a pickle. The fact is that, as best we can tell, everyone followed the plan appropriately—yet the team still failed. The leader set the schedule. There was no process for updating the schedule based on changing circumstances, and the delivery person followed the schedule. It's only when we look at the problem from the standpoint of a Level 3 Analysis that we recognize that the leader built an insufficient plan, one that didn't account for changes after the schedule was set. Our 5 Whys uncovered this, as did our Level 3 Analysis guide. The combination of the two sets the stage for what's to follow.

Having uncovered this fact, the analysis is not complete until we analyze the second potential Driving Factor. The dialogue might have continued as:

Leader: *So, gents, please tell me what happened with the blown fuse. Let's start with how it happened.*

Cook #1: *Sam and I were bored and were curious about some of the equipment that's sitting around the kitchen that we don't use. I guess we plugged in a few too many gadgets and blew a fuse.*

Leader: *OK. I understand how the fuse was blown. Talk me through what you did next.*

Cook #2: *Well, we decided to try to find the fuse box and reset the breaker. While we were trying to do that we got side-tracked a bit because the game was playing on my phone and it went into overtime. Playoff time and everything...I guess we got distracted and stopped looking for the box for a while.*

Leader: *Understood. Let me ask you this: how many calls came in during the time the oven wasn't at the right temperature?*

Cook #1: *None. We got lucky, I guess, but it was before dinner time and that was part of the reason we allowed ourselves to get sidetracked.*

Leader: *Got it. One final question: did you think to come find me and ask me where the fuse box is located?*

Cook #2:   *We did, but we really didn't want to bother you because we knew you were working on payroll and taxes. That stuff's important!*

When we look at this dialogue in terms of the objectives, we can see that the 55 minutes without power did nothing to affect delivery times because luckily no calls came in. That said, there's still a lesson to be learned; and potentially, changes to policy, plans and procedures that need to be made. The leader might quickly summarize in this way:

▶   Why did the kitchen lose power for 55 minutes? *Because the cooks decided to play with the equipment they didn't usually use, leading to a blown fuse.*

▶   Why didn't the cooks solve the problem sooner? *Because they got distracted playing on their phones, watching the game. In addition, they didn't want to interrupt their boss while he was working.*

▶   Why didn't they feel the sense of urgency to correct the problem? *Because there were no inbound calls or orders, and it was a quiet time in the kitchen. In addition, neither cook felt the internal sense of urgency to be proactive about the problem.*

▶ Why don't the cooks have an inherent sense of urgency? *Likely because they aren't fully vested in the work they're doing. They do what needs to be done, and that's the extent of their commitment.*

▶ Why aren't the cooks fully vested? *This is unclear and may be beyond the scope of where the leader wants to take this discussion. It may be that making a process change will be sufficient to address the issue without making more of this than need be. The leader may choose to dive deeper later, once this issue has passed and after taking time to observe the dynamics. This is the leader's call entirely.*

Addressing a Focus Point. Armed with this analysis, the leader can choose his approach for dealing with this issue. The challenge he has is that no harm was directly done; because of good fortune, there were no orders during the 55 minutes when the pizza joint was unable to make pizza. As such, the leader needs to be careful how he addresses this issue. He has to be aware of his team's perception of the event (nothing bad happened), the fact that he depends on his team to function, and that his team isn't as vested as he is in how the company operates (reference Patrick Lencioni's book *The Truth About Employee Engagement* for a perfect explanation of how to address this issue, and then read Les Landes' book *Getting to the Heart of Employee Engagement* for a deeper dive). A good option would be to ask his team for their thoughts on how effective they were and what steps they might take next time to avoid a potential problem.

Direct dialogue is likely the best step in this case to 1) correctly identify the core problems; 2) agree upon the solution to the problems; and 3) create "buy-in." Because this issue didn't end up hurting the team, it's wise of the leader to build buy-in through dialogue, as opposed to delivering his thoughts from the "top-down." Then, once the dialogue arrives at the logical conclusions, he could summarize in this way:

Leader: *OK, great discussion. And since this issue is not going to be part of our Root Cause analysis, let me just summarize what you guys said in our recap. I'll start by re-affirming that I'm glad, first of all, that you guys got it figured out in the end! Also, I'm glad nobody got hurt, despite the fact that some of that equipment was left over from the days when this place was a butcher's shop. I'll make a point of selling off the unnecessary equipment, but for now, I think we've agreed none of us will ever touch that stuff again!*

In addition, we recognize we got lucky. Despite the fact that we weren't able to produce pizzas for about an hour and 15 minutes (based on the oven's heating time once we got power back), we didn't lose any business. That's critical, and we dodged a bullet. Now, let's talk about what we can learn from this:

Moving forward, we've all agreed we're not going to be experimenting when we're bored. We'll instead spend our time looking at ways to improve our processes, to include making better, tastier pizzas. We've agreed to be pro-active, and not idle. [People-focused]

In addition, if we do run into a problem that affects business, we all agree that the first step is letting me know! It's pointless for me to be worried about taxes when we're not generating revenue, and I know more about this place than anyone here. I'm also going to find some time, when we're slow, to teach you more about our shop and to equip you for the day when I'm not here, so YOU can address the issues faster. [Mission-focused]

Finally, we've all agreed we're going to watch where our attention is focused. Even on slow days we can suddenly get slammed. If we're so caught up in the game, for example, so much so that we fail to prioritize getting the job done, we're failing ourselves. For now, we've agreed that we can keep listening to the games in the future; but, if they become distracting to business again, we'll have to revisit our policy. [Process-focused]

In less than five minutes the leader focused on what happened, and the team is potentially on a path to improvement. He communicated what he expects to be done, prioritized with People, Mission, and then Process. That said, just saying these words doesn't amount to anything; he and his team need to take actions have to be taken to verify that something has improved, and that they've learned lessons effectively. We'll address this more in a bit.

Now, back to the determination of which Driving Factor is the "Root Cause" of our missed objective. In this case, the first step would be to change the actual Driving Factor (DF), based on the additional inputs from the "perspective" questions we asked Tom. We would adjust the board as follows:

FQ: WHY WERE WE ONLY 75% EFFECTIVE AT DELIVERING ON-TIME PIZZAS?

> **DF: I NEED TO UPDATE THE SCHEDULE BASED ON REAL-TIME CHANGES**
>
> **DF: THE COOKS BLEW A FUSE LEADING TO A LOSS OF POWER FOR 55 MINUTES.**

STEP 5: Organize a plan to improve or maintain success.

As the driver noted, he arrived at work as per the schedule, at the time that was assigned. The leader needs to take ownership of this fact, adjust the Driving Factor accordingly, and develop the appropriate Fix.

A great technique is to draw a line through those Driving Factors that don't answer our question and identify the Root Cause with an arrow:

FQ: WHY WERE WE ONLY 75% EFFECTIVE AT DELIVERING ON-TIME PIZZAS?

> **—> DF: I NEED TO UPDATE THE SCHEDULE BASED ON REAL-TIME CHANGES**
>
> ~~**DF: THE COOKS BLEW A FUSE, LEADING TO A LOSS OF POWER FOR 55 MINUTES.**~~

One of the positive attributes of implementing this process is that by virtue of re-directing the potential root cause from Tom to himself, the leader gets to publicly take responsibility for an action that everyone else already knows was *his* mistake—but were uncomfortable highlighting because the leader is the "boss." By publicly undergoing the accountability process and outlining how he will personally change his processes to make life better for everyone, he gains credibility with his workers, credibility that would otherwise be very hard to come by. The BEST leaders in the world hold themselves accountable for their actions and highlight their mistakes openly, and right away. I've personally found that this methodology endears subordinates to their superiors, builds trust and creates a climate where people will go above and beyond the call of duty to support their accountable leadership.

STEP 6: Rapidly improve by memorializing.

This process concludes with the formal documentation of the debrief outcomes for future reference. The Pizza Shop may choose to go with the binder approach, capturing these lessons so that employees 1) act on and 2) apply them in the future. It's that easy.

Most importantly, **remember to end the debrief on a positive note,** *highlighting how close the team was to achieving success.* This is not an artificial effort; this is truly an opportunity to apply critical thinking to determine that success (if it wasn't attained) was within reach, and with a relatively simple fix will indeed be achieved the next time around. Making the debrief a positive experience will help drive interest in future experiences, which can only help the team grow stronger.

Partial Case Studies

I'll begin the next two "Partial Case Studies" by qualifying that we do not have access to all of the data we'd like to have in either example. In addition, and critically, we are relying on third-party sources in at least one case, and pure conjecture in the other, to arrive at our conclusions. You might be asking, "Why, then, are we looking at these examples?" The answer is simple: the core logic, as well as the conclusions we're going to arrive at, are worthy of our time, and we're only going to spend a little bit here. In addition, this is often the way we have to approach the problems with which we're faced—we don't have all of the data and yet we're required to make a decision. In this case, we'll make it easier on ourselves by focusing on the process rather than the outcomes.

I'll set these two examples up by providing the search terms you will find useful on YouTube to paint a background picture. Both videos take less than four minutes to watch. Next, I'll provide a quick summary of the facts that we have access to. Again, I'm not worried about the specifics because neither example is our immediate concern—I've picked these because they are good, quick and interesting studies for us to explore to help drive home a couple of points.

2017 Academy Awards

The first partial example we'll explore is from the 2017 Academy Awards. Those who watched this ceremony will likely recall that the last award of the night—the Best Picture Award—was presented to the wrong film. The team behind the film "La La Land" was called to the stage and was in the process of giving acceptance speeches when they were informed of the glaring mistake. A good summary of this event as it unfolded is available on YouTube; go to the YouTube search bar and type in "What Happened At The Oscars: Anatomy Of A Disaster" and click on the first video that pops up; it should be from NBC's "Today Show." The clip highlights the following events that took place (where "PWC" stands for Price Waterhouse Cooper):

- ▶ PWC Partner #1 was seemingly distracted just before handing out the final envelope, tweeting pictures backstage between awards

- ▶ PWC partner #1 handed the wrong award envelope to Presenter #1

- ▶ Presenter #1 noticed a discrepancy with the award card but was confused as to what to do

- ▶ Presenter #1 effectively handed the problem off to Presenter #2

- ▶ Presenter #2 immediately saw what she was looking for (the name of a film) and announced a winner

- ▶ Presenter #2 announced "La La Land" as the Best Picture winner, when the winner was actually "Moonlight"

► It took several minutes before the producer/team arrived on stage to correct the problem

► The correct winner, "Moonlight," was finally announced, 3+ minutes into the process

In keeping with the RAPTOR Debrief methodology, we begin by guessing the Objective for the 2017 Academy Awards. My personal guess is that the Objective looked like this:

OBJECTIVE: *"Host a fun, entertaining, and error-free Academy Awards ceremony."*

Based on this Objective, an initial glance at our very brief reconstruction would suggest a clear FQ:

FQ: WHY DID THE ACADEMY AWARD GO TO THE WRONG PICTURE?

This question sets us up to determine our Driving Factors. Again, we don't have access to much information, and the information we do have is from a third-party source. That said, there's more than enough data here to do some basic analysis, and to drive home a point about Root Cause determination.

To begin with, what's your take on this? From the information in the YouTube clip, summarized above, what do *you* think caused this mistake? Potential Driving Factors include the fact that PWC Partner #1 handed the wrong envelope to Presenter #1, which may have been a symptom of his distraction with the back-stage tweets. At the same time, Presenter #1 seems to have noticed the problem—his effort (or lack thereof) could well be a Driving Factor. Presenter #2 looks to have been trying to get the show back on-track after the delay in announcement from her partner. It makes sense that her part in this should be considered a Driving Factor. And then there's the production team, led by the PWC Partners who are the only ones who know the winners, having memorized the full list of winners prior to the event. The fact that it took several minutes before they responded is another Driving Factor for consideration.

And now to the reasons why we're using this example: there are two points I think are fundamental in the debrief process. The first is that the Root Cause of our problems is often not on our board in the form of our Reconstruction statements. Many times, the Root Cause needs to be derived by way of the critical thinking we discussed earlier; the entire process needs to be reviewed, effectively asking "Why" several times until we hit home. In this case I would ask:

▸ "Why did Presenter #2 feel like she needed to quickly offer a winner?" My guess is that the answer would be that she felt like her partner was dragging the process out, and that it was up to her to get the award out as quickly as possible.

▸ To this I would ask, "Why did Presenter #1 take so long, look around like he did, and ultimately not announce the winner, instead handing the envelope to Presenter #2?" My guess is that he realized he had the wrong results. He just didn't know what to do about it.

▶ This leads to two questions, the first being, "Why did Presenter #1 have the wrong envelope?" To which I would guess that PWC Partner #1 made a mistake. I have no reason to believe that PWC Partner #1 intentionally did what he did, though we should, in all fairness to the process, consider this possibility.

▶ But we'll assume that nothing intentional happened along those lines, which then leads to the question, "Why did PWC Partner #1 make this mistake?" And to this I would say, "I have no idea, aside from the fact that humans are prone to error."

▶ Returning to the second question about Presenter #1 getting the wrong envelope—my second question would be, "Why didn't Presenter #1 know what to do when he saw the mistake?" The answer to this question is tied to the Root Cause of the entire issue: The PLAN was flawed from the start in two specific ways.

First, **The Plan** does not seem to have accounted for the fact that *humans make mistakes*. As such, there was no fail-safe that we are aware of. Each PWC Partner was wholly responsible for correctly selecting and handing off the correct envelope to whichever presenter came their way. If the team running the show had wanted to avoid catastrophe, their plan needed to account for human error.

Second, *The Plan* does not seem to have prepared the key stakeholders for contingencies. On a stage and platform where Presenter #1 was being watched by millions of people around the globe, my assessment is that he froze. I'd say that the entire team was slow to react because they weren't rehearsed in how to address these kinds of mistakes. It is doubtful that anyone practiced the error protocols, even though it seems that two of the key stakeholders—specifically PWC Partners #1 and 2—were both aware of what should have happened.

> **MY QUICK SUMMARY WOULD BE TO SAY THAT THE OVERALL PLAN WAS NOT CORRECT FOR THE CIRCUMSTANCES**

My quick summary would be to say that the overall plan was not correct for the circumstances. The organizers may have defined the possibility of human error as an "acceptable risk," but the end result says this was not the correct approach; the whole ceremony builds up to the top award of the night and handing the final Academy Award to the wrong picture is an unacceptable and completely preventable error. That said, humans are prone to error and in order to avoid an award catastrophe, the plan should have been constructed to account for human error.

Without knowing any more of the details, I would propose as a Fix that future ceremonies only allow presenters to come from one side of the stage, that the two PWC Partners do a physical double-check of each envelope. I would also propose that the producer be made aware of the results in advance. In addition, I would further propose that future teams rehearse error correction protocols with everyone involved, to include the presenters, so that the contingency plan could happen more efficiently.

All of this said, our analysis hinges on what I proposed as the stated or implied Objective for the show. Now think of this—what if the Objective I proposed was wrong? This brings me to my second reason for using this example: *Knowing the Objective is critical to the process.* In this case, I assume that the organizers wanted to "Host a fun, entertaining, and error-free Academy Awards ceremony," but what if that's an incorrect assumption? If the Objective was secretly to create a situation that keeps the Academy Awards in the public consciousness for weeks and months after the event, they achieved their goal and then some. If that was the case, then I take back everything I've written and offer kudos to the organizers for doing a brilliant job!

Mr. Smith's (Former Equifax CEO's) Testimony to Congress

The second example I'd like to highlight comes from the former Equifax CEO, Mr. Smith's, testimony to Congress about the massive data breach that took place in 2017. The full testimony is far too long for our purposes, and the most important part for what we're looking to explore is captured in a short clip. Again, the search terms for your YouTube search are as follows: "Former Equifax CEO Richard Smith: Criminal Hack On My Watch And I Take Full Responsibility." This video clip is from CNBC and is just shy of four minutes.

What's interesting is that there is neither a Reconstruction, nor much in the way of Driving Factor development. Mr. Smith essentially cuts to the chase and offers his Root Cause analysis for the world to hear and evaluate. Here's what I took from this clip:

▶   The former CEO accepts full responsibility for what happened (Level 3 effort);

▶   The Root Causes he identifies are: 1) Human Error, in that someone (an individual) didn't install a vital system patch, and 2) Technical Error, in that the monitoring systems didn't catch the fact that the patch wasn't installed (Level 2 analysis).

This should be pretty cut-and-dry. The CEO, who resigned his position after millions of people across the globe had their personal data stolen in one of the worst data breaches in the world to-date, took *full responsibility* for what happened. He provided the U.S. Congress with two Root Causes for the breach, ostensibly after his team did their full Root Cause analysis. What more could we possibly want?

I share this example because I believe Mr. Smith really meant what he said. I also think he and his team believe that they identified the correct Root Causes of the breach and, in a way, they sort of did. Most importantly, I also believe that with a little training, everyone on the Equifax team would have recognized the inadequacy of their conclusions and probed further.

Once again, the *plan* is the area that seems to be the one most likely to need additional work, and Mr. Smith should have outlined how he failed to lead effectively by allowing a bad plan to help safeguard so much sensitive data. His assumption of full responsibility for the problem was an insufficient response, especially in light of the fact that 143+ million people had their personal data fall into the hands of nefarious individuals. Let's look at this through the 5 Whys approach:

► Why did 143M+ people across the globe have their personally-identifiable information stolen? *Because human error led to someone not installing a necessary patch. Because the technical systems didn't catch the fact that the patch wasn't installed.*

► Why didn't the human properly install the patch? *We don't know.*

► Why didn't the technical system catch the error? *We don't know.*

► Why was the security of 143M+ people in the hands of what looks to have been one human, backed up by a technical scanner? *We don't know.*

► Why weren't more people involved in the setup and implementation of the security patch? *We don't know.*

There's clearly a lot that we don't know, but looking at the question through this perspective highlights something that doesn't seem right: there's probably too much responsibility heaped on one person to say that this single person's error is the root cause of the problem. Let's apply the Appreciation approach here and see what we come up with:

▶ One person is responsible for ensuring the necessary patches are installed to safeguard the private information of over 143M people.

So what?

▶ So this means that this person better be at work every day, better make sure they're aware of what needs to be installed, etc.

So what?

▶ So we're going to need to make sure that there's a plan in place, in the event he or she doesn't make it to work or makes a mistake.

So what?

▶ So the plan needs to consider contingencies like the sort I just highlighted, and build in appropriate mitigations.

So what?

▶ So our current contingency plan relies on an automated scanner to ensure everything is done correctly.

So what?

▶ So we probably need to have someone double-checking that the automated scanner is working, to make sure we're truly OK.

Since we're still lacking sufficiency with the Appreciation approach, we'll return to the Level 3 Analysis guide. Here we get to some compelling questions:

LEVEL 3 ANALYSIS DRIVING FACTORS / FOCUS AREAS

GUIDANCE

- *Was the plan the right one?*

- *Was it sufficient to address the needs for the entirety of execution?*

- *Did the plan include enough detail to address the challenges we faced?*

- *Did the plan sufficiently address contingencies?*

- *Was the plan executable based on the skills and expertise of the team?*

I know we don't have all of the information Mr. Smith and his team had. But I also firmly believe that what we really expected during Mr. Smith's testimony was a satisfying answer, and I don't believe that the two Root Causes presented are sufficient. I believe that The plan was at fault in this case as well, for two reasons: 1) placing the security of almost 150 million people's data in the hands of one person, who must install a patch correctly and in a timely fashion, seems a risky proposition, even with a scanner backup—it doesn't seem sufficient to address the core need; and 2) whenever the blame for a massive error stops at a low-level practitioner, the identified Root Cause is usually not a Level 3 Root Cause. It is therefore an insufficient answer from the perspective of someone practicing full Accountable Leadership. Any time a leader accepts responsibility but doesn't offer how it is that he could have done a better job, how he or she failed the team, we have to probe further.

> **I BELIEVE THAT THE PLAN WAS AT FAULT IN THIS CASE AS WELL**

This is a critically important point for leaders who want to start practicing Accountable Leadership. Leaders build and approve plans, so they're the ones who ultimately benefit when plans are run successfully—they reap the rewards, even if they don't fully understand the plans. But, just like we identified with the captain of the ship that crashed into the other, or the pilots and aircrew who shot down the Blackhawk helicopters in Iraq—it's also the leaders who need to take ownership of plans that *don't* turn out well, to include explaining what they would have done differently, based on the results. I believe that a well-intentioned Mr. Smith failed to do this adequately, even if he tried to do the right thing.

The good news is that the correction only needs to be very minor to have the right effect. If Mr. Smith had stated that the person failed to install the update, the scanner failed to catch the mistake, but ultimately the plan was at fault because it depended too heavily on an inadequate safeguarding system, he would have been on to something. Furthermore, if he had offered that he should have implemented a plan that took full advantage of the IT safeguarding team in place (he was personally responsible for increasing the size of the security staff at Equifax), outlining some of the key areas where they could have done good work, I believe his testimony would have been both correct and fully satisfying. It's a small tweak, but it makes a world of difference in terms of the outcome.

CHAPTER 8

"PARTING SHOTS"

SUCCESS IS A SCIENCE; IF YOU HAVE THE
CONDITIONS, YOU GET THE RESULT.

Oscar Wilde

A Quick Personal Example

We've covered the key components of how to run an effective debrief, as well as outlined a practical, simple example of a debrief in a business context. We've also looked at some pointed, albeit brief case studies of relatively recent events to highlight the importance of the plan, in terms of Root Cause analysis. I'd like to now circle back to the issue of psychological safety and share a quick story from my time as the commander of the 7th Fighter Squadron.

In the Spring of 2010, I took command of the "Screamin' Demons" as we were known, and immediately started preparing to deploy the squadron from New Mexico to Okinawa, Japan. We were tasked to deploy for four months, and we had a LOT of work to do in a very short period to get ready for our tasking. I was simultaneously learning to fly the F-22 as well as dealing with the challenges of a new command. I had just a couple of months to get things ready for our squadron to take part in its first-ever trans-oceanic deployment. I had a lot on my mind.

All of this came to a disturbing head one day when I was flying a mission and realized that I was not at all focused on my flying. I put myself and my airplane in a touchy situation, and I felt like I had momentarily lost control of my airplane. In the debrief, I took a look at the "lineup card" we use to document critical data for the flight and recognized that I had taken plenty of notes during the mission briefing. The problem was that NONE of these notes had ANYTHING to do with the mission we were about to fly. My card was full of scribble tied exclusively to our upcoming deployment. I shared with my instructor that my mind was nowhere near the mission; I was focused almost exclusively on the administrative tasks we needed to handle to be ready to deploy, and I was putting myself and my formation at risk as a result.

As I sat there thinking things through, I realized that I was setting a horrible example. The only way I knew to correct my poor example was to ground myself, and so I did. I called the squadron together and shared with them what had taken place, how my focus was nowhere near where it needed to be. And then I told everyone that I was grounding myself for a week. I briefed my team on the recovery plan I instituted for myself, one that included study time, an emergency procedures simulator with an instructor, and then a return-to-fly program that was both practical, as well as incredibly humbling. I was open, forthright, and sincere. And I think the squadron both understood and appreciated why I did what I did.

Why do I share this? Only because it was one way in which I used the power of debrief for what I hoped would be the betterment of my organization as a whole. I shared the outcome—my complete lack of focus on my core mission task of flying—so that everyone could see that 1) *we all* make mistakes; 2) even though we acknowledge our mistakes, we're still held accountable for our decisions and NOBODY is immune to that; 3) there *is* a way to recover; and 4) I knew I needed a kick in the pants to get myself back on-track.

I will say that the feedback I received both from my subordinates, as well as my boss, was all positive. I believe that episode was a good one, especially for my organization at its particular stage of development (we were a brand-new squadron at the time). If I had to do that event over again, I certainly would.

When Do We Debrief?

This is a really easy question to answer because of its simplicity: we debrief every time we complete an event, whether that event is a sales call, a management action, or whatever. It doesn't matter if the event happens once a day, once a week, once a month or once a year. In the flying world, we debriefed after every single mission; in the business world, we debrief after every single event. We do this for two reasons. The first is that we need to have a solid recall of the facts. The longer we go between the event and the reconstruction, the less-accurate our results will be, unless we each take outstanding notes (which is occasionally but not *usually* the case).[93] The second is that we need to get into the habit of debriefing, which will take time to develop. The only way to make this a habit is to start doing debriefs after every single event.

I recognize that this can initially be difficult to implement. The institutional antibodies—the people who are stubbornly resistant to a new process—are going to fight you. The folks who are comfortable with the status quo aren't going to want to accept the change, especially when it might mean exposing areas to review that don't usually get exposed. Regular debriefing can also be difficult if you're used to bringing in an outside facilitator to run your debriefs—availability might be an issue, and there's also the concern of whether it's feasible to rely on an outsider to constantly run debriefs inside your organization.

And so, I say again: your leaders should run your debriefs. It's that plain and simple. And you should debrief *every time you finish an event*. In the business world, we have plenty of events that warrant debriefs. A starting point for determining what to debrief includes the following considerations:

▶ Did you build and then execute a plan? If so, debrief.

▶ Did you execute something, even if you didn't have a plan? If so, debrief.

▶ Did you just experience something that didn't go as envisioned or planned? If so, debrief what happened.

▶ Did you encounter something new / strange / different? If so, debrief what happened.

Your default approach should be to debrief *more often than not*, and to begin training debrief practitioners in your organization who are capable of leading your teams to success. You should identify your early adopters along with your most-skilled practitioners and make them the institutional experts who help lead the transition. Most importantly, if you're the leader, YOU should be guiding everyone else, practicing debriefs on a regular basis and bringing your teams with you.

How Do We Overcome Institutional Antibodies?

For this, I'll turn to the work of Tannenbaum and Cerasoli, researchers who have been studying debriefs for a long time. They conclude that the data clearly says to do it. Specifically, and as

highlighted in a recent article in People + Strategy, "Well-con-
ducted debriefs work, and there is strong meta-analytic evidence to support that contention. A meta-analysis is a statis-
tical combination of all prior empirical studies on a topic. We
generally have more confidence in the findings from a meta-analysis than from any one
study. Tannenbaum and Cerasoli conducted a meta-analysis
of 46 prior research samples
that examined debriefing. On
average, teams that conduct debriefs outperform those that do
not by over 20 percent. That's a
remarkable bump for a relatively simple intervention."[93]

> **RESEARCH INDICATES THAT TEAMS THAT CONDUCT EFFECTIVE DEBRIEFS OUTPERFORM OTHER TEAMS BY AN AVERAGE OF 25%**

From a white paper by
the Group for Organizational
Research Effectiveness (gOE),
"Research indicates that teams
that conduct effective debriefs
outperform other teams by an
average of 25%."[94] In addition, it is "among the most cost-effec-
tive ways of promoting on-going learning and ensuring team
effectiveness."[95] Think of what this means to your organization.
Consider the implications, especially if you're already performing at a high-level. Imagine improving by another 25+ percent
at the cost of spending time with your teams!

Interestingly, this data doesn't come from the military.

For reference, Scott Tannenbaum is the President of the Group for Organizational Effectiveness (gOE), which is a consulting and research firm that focuses much of its attention on debriefing. He's devoted an entire line of business towards getting organizations to embrace the power of the debrief. Dr. Eduardo Salas (co-author of the People+Strategy article) is the Allyn R. & Gladys M. Cline Chair Professor and Chair of the Department of Psychology at Rice University. He's also the father of TeamSTEPPS®, the program I outlined earlier, which builds on the U.S. Navy's approach to Crew Resource Management to help mitigate risk in the healthcare environment. His version of debriefing is used across the globe, because he learned long ago that high-performing military teams know how to do this better than anyone else.

The point here is simple: don't take *my* word for it; those who have studied it recognize that debriefing is extremely effective, and you have plenty of sources to cite when being asked to offer "proof." Those organizations who embrace it (and many are trying to) are experiencing incredible results. If your organization wants to become as good as it can be, it should consider implementing high-quality debriefs.

The Debrief as a Tool for Performance Evaluations

When we view debriefing as a tool, it's clear that we can use it in a variety of ways. One obvious derivative is to use this tool for Performance Evaluations. Leaders/managers frequently struggle with the correct way to evaluate their people. The debrief is an outstanding tool for leaders to use *to have the difficult conversations about performance* that might otherwise not go so well. In the flying world, we use versions of this tool to evaluate our people all the way from pilot training through Weapons School. In an evaluation context, once the core debrief is complete the rest of the formation is cleared off (in the case of more than a 2-ship). The Instructor Pilot (IP)—armed with the data from the debrief—can now evaluate that person's performance. Here are some of the things we did in the evaluation portion of missions:

▶ We used a grade sheet and tracked performance on every item listed;

▶ The IP awarded a grade for every element under evaluation;

▶ The IP awarded an overall grade, which meant the difference between passing and failing;

▶ Grade sheets became part of every pilot's formal record. I have copies of the grade sheets for almost all of my flying throughout my career. Some are comical. Some remind me of awesome missions. And some, quite the opposite!

The exact same approach can work well for performance evaluations in an organizational context. These can be accomplished either as a part of an existing debrief or as a stand-alone event between the leader / manager and the employee. The process remains the same. Consider the implications and recognize the advantages of bringing this to bear on an HR level.

How Do We Get to the Level We Need to with Debriefs?

To begin with, you're going to need a local expert who is qualified to lead debriefs. Note that I say *qualified*, and not *certified*. Certifications, in my humble opinion, are insufficient in tracking an individual's capability to perform a given task. They're often nothing more than proof of attendance, and the problem is that they don't require demonstrations of skill. A qualification, on the other hand, is earned by proving one's abilities to a qualified evaluator. In order to become a debrief instructor, I had to become qualified to teach debriefing. This is what sets me apart in the business world.

> IT'S SIMPLE TO GET QUALIFIED: ALL YOU HAVE TO DO IS ATTEND A VMAX GROUP QUALIFICATION COURSE **"**

You need to become qualified to lead a debrief, *and* you need to find early adopters in your organization who can also become qualified. Leadership by example is vitally important, and as uncomfortable as some leaders may be at learning and practicing this process (it may take people well outside of their comfort zone), it is critical that leaders adopt and practice this skill first. Once they've demonstrated the capability, they then need to hold their teams accountable for adopting and practicing this skill as well. Reyes, Tannenbaum and Salas note that "With expanding spans of control, most leaders can't see everything that is going on in their team. If team members don't have a vehicle for sharing what they are seeing, the leader and other team members are operating partially in the dark. Periodic debriefs help turn on the light."[97] In other words, show your leaders and colleagues what they gain by this, lead them through the process yourself, and change your organizational DNA for the better. 20+% improvement starts NOW!

It's simple to get qualified: all you have to do is attend a VMax Group qualification course. We're building courses and developing an ongoing schedule to support you across the U.S. and across the globe all year through. We're available to come into your organization and teach you and your teams directly. We're engaging and our feedback and reviews are world-class. The purpose of our Debrief course is to teach you how to successfully lead debriefs of your own, enabling you to become the resident expert in your organization. Once you're qualified, you'll need to maintain your qualifications through regular practice, something we'll emphasize in the course. You'll also need to stretch yourself by seeking out and dealing with tough debrief scenarios with peers and above. The good news is that once learned, the skill is a life skill that will serve you well in *everything you do*, not just business. When you're ready to learn more, feel free to drop us a line at info@vmaxgroupllc. com. You can also call us at 1-800-455-3122. We look forward to speaking with you, learning more about you, and offering you help in applying this approach in your organization!

CONCLUSION

"

IF YOUR ACTIONS INSPIRE OTHERS TO
DREAM MORE, LEARN MORE, DO MORE
AND BECOME MORE, YOU ARE A LEADER.

John Quincy Adams

Every year lots of people tune in to watch Charles Dickens' "A Christmas Carol." Why? I think it's because Dickens penned a powerful story about *conversion*—of someone recognizing we're all on our way to some final reckoning, and how we live along the way actually matters. The character of Ebenezer Scrooge is presented with a reconstruction of his past, a perspective of his present, and a glimpse of his future, if he stays on his current course. Needless to say, Mr. Scrooge isn't too excited by what he sees. He's not satisfied with the outcome of this *personal debrief*. He wisely elects to do something with the time he has left, in order to become someone better—*and does it*! This is the hook that keeps people coming back, the realization that, with life there's time to change, and the debrief is the powerful tool that enables this type of conversion.

Debrief to Win is obviously about the importance of accountability in leadership, and the way in which we can practice this and simultaneously build great teams, by way of high quality debriefs. And while we're not concentrating on personal conversions, the approach offered to Scrooge is a great one for us to consider in our companies and organizations. Imagine for one moment that you were able to reconstruct what your organization has previously done, and then look carefully at what it is currently doing. Then imagine what it would look like if you were able to see some distance off in the future—where would your organization be? What level of success will you have attained? How happy will you and your employees be?

While I realize that we don't have this direct capability, we do have the ability to forecast and to scan the environment. We can look at micro and macro trends, and we can see what our competitors are doing. And then we can ask ourselves preemptively: "If we were to debrief ourselves at some point in the future, what conclusions would we draw about our performance today?" Sometimes, this kind of analysis sheds light into areas we can change right now. Sometimes it helps us to re-direct our efforts in a better direction. Maybe it's something you can do in your organization today.

I really enjoyed teaching during my flying days; I was privileged to do a lot of it both in the air and in the classroom. Now I get to do it in the corporate world by way of VMax Group and joint ventures like Next-Generation Edge™ and "Top Gun CEO Bootcamp." It turns out that teaching in the corporate world is JUST AS MUCH FUN as in the flying world—perhaps even a little more so, because our corporate clients are recognizing the power of the RAPTOR Debrief for the very first time. They're overwhelmed as they begin to appreciate its value and apply it to their businesses and lives. They see the value as their teams start to perform better and do things they were not able to do before.

My sincere hope is that you, too, see the tremendous value in implementing *Accountable Leadership* by way of the RAPTOR Debrief in your company or organization. My hope is that you choose to invest your time in bringing it to life in your business and in your personal life. In saying this I'll turn to fellow author Chet Richards, author of *Certain to Win*, and share his wise words of caution with you:

> *"You can't blame people for wanting instant results. Time is money, and quickness...is good...for some reason, otherwise intelligent people sometimes feel they should be able to attend a three-day seminar and return home experts in maneuver conflict as applied to business. An intensive orientation session may get you started, but successful leaders study their art for years—Patton, Rommel, and Grant were all know for the intensity with which they studied military history and current campaigns."[98]*

It's going to take time to implement the Debrief as a part of your organization's DNA, so please don't be discouraged if it doesn't suddenly "click" the first time you try it.

That said, early on in this process I received a text from

a very successful business principal who, following an introductory overview meeting only four days prior, started implementing the full *Debrief-Focused Approach*™ in his business. These are his complete and unsolicited words:

> *"I've used that framework of objective, plan, who needs to understand the plan multiple times since our last meeting and people look at me like I'm a genius! It's amazing how we lose track of how to do effective accountability. It's also crazy how many ways and places it is great to use."*

I didn't ask for his feedback; he reached out to me out of excitement. He shared this because of his enthusiasm for what we're doing by way of The Debrief-Focused Approach™. My wish is that you feel the same way.

VMax Group, is here to assist you in implementing both Debriefs and The Debrief-Focused Approach™ in your organization. VMax Group's mission is to train and coach you on how to apply these methodologies to your business and, by extension, your life. We will do everything we can to meet you where you are, to help you succeed by way of Accountability, Leadership and Teamwork. Let's get started on making you the best version of you there is!

I hope you enjoyed Debrief to Win and, if you did, please stay tuned for my next book, "Team to Succeed."

APPENDIX

DEBRIEF VOCABULARY

B ack in 2004, I started my work as the Subject Matter Expert on Debriefing at the USAF Weapons School. Little did I know then that the paper I would write in 2005—titled *The Vocabulary of the Debrief*, and published in the 2005 Summer edition of the *Weapons School Review*— would literally define the terms that would be used across the Air Force from that point forward. Indeed, the terms we defined in that paper are still in use across the force today. I did appreciate the need for uniformity and standardization as we were working hard at that time to work cross-functionally across disciplines. But the terms I used amounted to more than merely "uniform" or "standardized" terms; they effectively defined the debriefing process. We were moving away from being compatible groups of individual teams to an interconnected and highly-lethal team of teams in how we executed the air battle. The first step of that inter-connectivity involved making sure we all spoke the same language.

My purpose in this short section is to provide definitions of some of the vocabulary you came across in this book. I've chosen to keep the military parlance when I teach this approach to businesses across the globe. This came to a head when a client advised me he was going to "de-militarize" some of the language on some of the materials I had prepared for him—and I recommended he not do that. I reminded him that he brought me in specifically to help him incorporate *The Debrief-Focused Approach* into his company's DNA. I advised him that I wasn't there to change my approach to make it conform to the status-quo—far from it. I reminded him that he asked for my help in order to embrace winning the way our front-line fighter squadrons win, and part of that means accepting and adopting new terminology. I'm happy to report that he's still a client and he's using our vocabulary.

Briefing: *An event where the leader of the team explains how the team is going to succeed at achieving the stated objectives. The briefing follows a regular flow and can be repeated.*

Checklist: *A document listing the necessary steps for completion of a given task.*

Commander's Intent: *A succinct description of what constitutes success for the operation as determined by the commander. It includes the operation's purpose, key tasks, and the conditions that define the end state. It links the mission, concept of operations, and tasks to subordinate units. A clear commander's intent facilitates a shared understanding and focuses on the overall conditions that represent mission accomplishment.[99]*

Continuation Training: *A mission, or an exercise, flown or conducted specifically for training. There is usually no upgrade or other purpose for the mission.*

Driving Factors: *Potential answers to our Fundamental Question.*

Fundamental Question: *The key question of the Debrief, usually phrased as "Why" the objective was or was not achieved.*

Goals: *Broad outcomes that drive strategy.*

Instructor Pilot (IP): *A pilot specifically qualified to teach some or all portions of a flying training syllabus.*

Memorialization: *The written summary of the results of a Debrief, performed at the very end of the process.*

Objectives: *The tool we use to help us achieve our Goals. These are achievable, measurable statements that are defined in time.*

Plan: *The way a team intends to achieve its objective(s), in support of its overall goals.*

Reconstruction: *The written summary of the events that happened during the execution of an event. The Reconstruction process helps drive the debrief by providing multiple perspectives of the truth of what happened.*

Root Cause: *The reason or reasons why an objective either was or was not achieved.*

Situational Awareness (SA): *Awareness of what's happening around you, "in order to understand how information, events, and your own actions will impact goals and objectives, both immediately and in the near-future."*[100]

Standards: *How a team sets out to perform its core tasks.*

Strategy: *The way in which Goals will be achieved.*

Tactics: *The means by which one achieves the stated objectives.*

Tactical Execution: *The part of the mission that is focused on achieving the stated objectives.*

Team: *"A small group of people (typically fewer than twenty) with complimentary skills committed to a common purpose and set of specific performance goals. Its members are committed to working with each other to achieve the team's purpose and hold each other fully and jointly accountable for the team's results.*[101]

Upgrade Ride: *A mission flown to achieve or demonstrate continued qualifications. Usually a high-pressure ride flown with either an Instructor or an Evaluator Pilot.*

ACKNOWLEDGEMENTS

This is the hard part—trying to thank everyone who had a role in bringing this book from concept to reality. I'll do my best, knowing that I will almost certainly miss someone along the way, which is in no way my intent.

To the several wonderful people who read through the original manuscript of *Debrief to Win*—the version centered on my walk with cancer and its surgical aftermath—a profound thank you! Specifically, to Eland Mann at Advantage Media, to Mr. Chet Richards, brilliant author of *Certain to Win*, and to my friend and one-time F-15 instructor, Colonel Lance "Blade" Wilkins, as well as to my brother and former U.S. Navy pilot, LCDR Anthony "Lennie" Teschner —my deepest appreciation for your time and interest, as well as your kind efforts to improve that version of this book. I am most of all thankful to Michael E. Gerber for your admittedly painful counsel that I "wrote the wrong book." This was not at all the answer I was looking for, and my respect for you is as high as it is because you didn't hesitate to give me the unvarnished truth. I always respect your advice, I'm honored to know you and have you on my side, and I re-wrote this book mostly from scratch, solely on your recommendation.

To the many who read the second version of the manuscript and offered your wisdom to make this project a success—my sincerest thanks as well! Specifically, I thank my Weapons School classmate and life-long friend, Lt Col (ret.) Rob "Brutus" Jackson; I thank the several members of the extended VMax Group team who provided validation of this approach, as well as direct feedback on the manuscript, to include Mr. Andrew Marks, whose experience and input as an engineer was an inspiration to me; Mr. Steve Young, whose validation as a former CEO and General Counsel had the same effect; and again Colonel Lance "Blade" Wilkins, fellow Weapons School alumnus and author; fellow National Defense University alumnus, Robert "FOG" Huntington; and my dear friend in the book business, Mr. John Lund. I'm thankful as well to Mr. Gabe Zubizarreta for caring enough to read multiple versions of the revised book, and to spend quality time outlining detailed thoughts and suggestions. I also appreciate the continued support of my friends Lt Col (ret.) Jeremy "Huck" Durtschi, and Col (ret.) Jim "High Drag" Ravella, as well as my cousin Michael Gillani.

In addition, I am thankful to my partner in, and co-founder of, Next-Generation Edge™, Mr. Brian "Ponch" Rivera, not only for your constant encouragement, but also for your excellent recommendations to bring critical elements of NGE™ into play in this manuscript. To Mr. Les Landes—thank you for your detailed corrections and for your continuous help in bringing *Debrief to Win* to the marketplace, as well as sharing your brilliant book *Getting to the Heart of Employee Engagement* with me—I'm a huge fan! And to the best of many outstanding squadron commanders I've ever served under, as well as one of my favorite people on the planet, Lt Col (ret.) Nick

"Neeck" Nichols—a very special word of thanks for your tremendous help and constant encouragement!

I'm also deeply grateful to the many instructors who taught me *The Art of the Debrief*, as well as the countless teammates who suffered through my own debriefs along the way. Specifically, I would like to thank Col (ret.) Terry "Stretch" Scott, Col (ret.) Brad "Tonto" Bird, Col (ret.) Mike "Gomez" King, Maj Gen Barry "Dawg" Cornish, Lt Col (ret.) Rob "Bam Bam" Martyn, Lt Col (ret.) Ken "Mach" Tatum, all of my Instructors at the USAF Weapons Instructor Course (WIC Class 02-BIN), as well as my WIC classmates, to specifically include Lt Col (ret.) Rob "Brutus" Jackson and Lt Col (ret.) Dave "Fester" Lynch (without whom our "Tactical Intercepts" debriefs would not have been nearly as much "fun"!). Perhaps most importantly, I thank all of those who suffered through my Weapons School-style debriefs during my time as a young Weapons Officer in the 27th Fighter Squadron at Langley AFB, VA. And I sincerely thank all of my students from Class 04-AIN through course 06-AIN at the USAF Weapons Instructor Course for helping me learn how to improve my debriefs at a place where there is zero room for error.

To my outstanding book development team—a HUGE word of thanks! I offer my gratitude to Mr. Larry Schweikart and Mr. Leon Pein for your work editing the core manuscript and aiding its readability. I am extremely thankful to Ms. Christine Moore of John Wiley & Sons for your care in polishing this manuscript in preparation for its international release! I thank Ms. Jenni Woodhead for your absolutely brilliant work designing the stunning interior layout of this book! I'm grateful to Mr. Alexander Vulchev for crafting an absolutely magnificent and unforgettable cover! And I offer a most special thank you to my dear sister-in-law for your care and dedication in proofing the final manuscript!

Thanks as well to Mr. Steve "Buick" Olds for originally introducing me to Mr. Gerber and for your words of encouragement on this special project. I offer my gratitude to Maj Gen (ret.) Joe Balskus for providing me both an opportunity and a stage on which to translate my story and its debrief into motivational speaking, one of the true joys of my new career! And I'm extremely grateful to Mr. Andy Marks for your financial gift to help bring this book to life, as well as to Mr. Steve Young for your standing offer to do the same!

Most of all, I thank my family for supporting me every step along the way. To my Mom and to my Mother and Father-in-Law—thank you for all you've done for me and my beautiful family, especially through cancer and beyond, and for believing in me and in my new purpose in life. To my brother Anthony—thank you for reading carefully (suffering?) through both versions of this book and for your outstanding and encouraging feedback in both cases. And to my beautiful bride Diane—your feedback, encouragement, support and love provided me all the motivation I needed to keep working and to get this book to the finish-line. I'll love you forever! And to my dearest children—THANK YOU for your patience with me while I've been working on this! I promise I'll make it up to you soon, hopefully after I finish writing the next book in this series, *Team to Succeed*!

ENDNOTES

1. Peterson, Hayley, Harney, Megan, and Tyler, Jessica. "Sears is shutting down 78 more stores. Here are all of the locations shutting down where you live." http://www.businessinsider.com/sears-stores-for-sale-2018-4, 2018.

2. Ibid.

3. Pfeffer, Jeffrey. Leadership BS: Fixing Workplaces and Careers One Truth at a Time. New York: HarperCollins, 2015 in Molinaro, Vince. The Leadership Contract. New Jersey: John C. Wiley & Sons, Inc., 2018, p.33.

4. Ibid, 33.

5. Ibid, 33.

6. Reyes, Tannenbaum, and Salas. "Team Development: The Power of Debriefing." People + Strategy, Spring 2018.

7. Eilertsen, Soren. The Nature of Business Tribes. April, 2018. https://www.clomedia.com/2018/04/16/nature-business-tribes/.

8. Molinaro, Vince. The Leadership Contract. New Jersey: John C. Wiley & Sons, Inc., 2018, 38.

9. Ibid., 39.

10. Ibid., 40.

11. Ibid., 28.

12. Ibid., 30.

13. Chandler, Alfred D. Visible Hand: The Managerial Revolution in American Business. Harvard: Belknap Press, 1977.

14. Molinaro, Vince. The Leadership Contract. New Jersey: John C. Wiley & Sons, Inc., 2018, 32.

15. Cokins, Gary. "Corporate Decision-Making: Why do large, once-successful companies fail?" http://analytics-magazine.org/corporate-decision-making-why-do-large-once-successful-companies-fail/, 2012.

16. Fraser, Alec. Damn the Torpedoes! Annapolis, MD: Naval Institute Press, 2016, 20.

17. Ibid, 27.

18. Koenigsaecker, George. Leading the Lean Enterprise Transformation. Boca Raton, FL: CRC Press, 2016, 88.

19. Schweikart, Larry and Lynne Pierson Doti, American Entrepreneur. New York: AMACOM Press, 2009, 325-27.

20. Pelissero, Tom. "Why do Patriots keep winning? Hall of Fame coaches explain Bill Belichick's success." USA Today online: https://www.usatoday.com/story/sports/nfl/patriots/2016/09/29/bill-belichick-new-england-jimmy-garoppolo-bill-parcells-tony-dungy/91282168/

21. Watts, Geoff. Scrum Mastery. Cheltenham, Glos: Inspect & Adapt, Ltd., 2013, 41.

22. Fussell, Chris. One Mission: How Leaders Build a Team of Teams. New York: Penguin Random House LLC., 2017, 36.

23. Merriam Webster's Collegiate Dictionary, Tenth Edition. Springfield, MA: Merriam-Webster, Incorporated, 1999, 297.

24. Rayder, John P.H. "Armed for Success: External Factors of the World War I Aces." U.S. Army Command and General Staff College, Ft Leavenworth, KS, 1995, 61.

25. Ibid., 77-78.

26. Ibid., 30.

27. Reyes, Tannenbaum, and Salas. "Team Development: The Power of Debriefing." People + Strategy, Spring 2018.

28. Collins, Jim. Good to Great. New York: HarperCollins Publishers Inc., 2001, 89.

29. Kerth, Norman. Project Retrospectives. New York, NY: Dorset House Publishing Co., Inc., 2001, xvi.

30. Willink, Jocko and Babin, Leif. Extreme Ownership. New York: St. Martin's Press, 2015, 206.

31. Shalev, Arieh M.D. "Historical Group Debriefing Following Combat." Hadassah University Center for Traumatic Stress, 1991, http://www.dtic.mil/dtic/tr/fulltext/u2/a247839.pdf.

32. Salas, Eduardo, Marissa L. Shuffler, Amanda L. Thayer, Wendy L. Bedwell, and Elizabeth H. Lazzara. "Understanding and Improving Teamwork in Organizations: A Scientifically Based Practical Guide". Human Resource Management, Wiley Periodicals, Inc., 2014, 2.

33. https://www.gvsu.edu/cms4/asset/CC22E6AB-DC19-6BE8-D720E30BBEEBBAD3/salas_-_miperc_presentation_final_9-21-17.pdf

34. Salas, E., Benishek, L., Coultas, C., Diets, A., Grossman, R., Lazzara, & E., Oglesby, J. Team training essentials: A research-based guide. New York: Routledge, 2015.

35. Loeffler, Marc. Improving Agile Retrospectives. Pearson Education, Inc., 2018.

36. Watts, Geoff. Scrum Mastery. Cheltenham, Glos: Inspect & Adapt, Ltd., 2013, 50.

37. Bussell, Daniel. The Anticipatory Organization. Austin, TX: Greenleaf Book Group Press, 2017, 109-110.

38. Fussell, Chris. One Mission: How Leaders Build a Team of Teams. New York: Penguin Random House LLC., 2017, 41.

39. Gerber, Michael E. Private conversation, 2018.

42. Edmondson, Amy. "Psychological Safety, Trust, and Learning in Organizations: A Group-level Lens. Trust and Distrust in Organizations: Dilemmas and Approaches," 2011.

43. Delizona, Laura. "High-Performing Teams Need Psychological Safety. Here's How to Create it." https://hbr.org/2017/08/high-performing-teams-need-psychological-safety-heres-how-to-create-it, 2017.

44. Ibid.

45. Ibid.

46. Edmondson, A. C. "Teaming: How organizations learn, innovate, and compete in the knowledge economy." New York: Josey-Bass, 2012.

47. Katzenbach, Jon R. and Smith, Douglas K. The Discipline of Teams. https://hbr.org/2005/07/the-discipline-of-teams, 2005.

48. Collins, Jim. Good to Great. New York: HarperCollins Publishers Inc., 2001, 74.

49. Coleman, John. "Six Components of a Great Corporate Culture." https://hbr.org/2013/05/six-components-of-culture, 2013.

50. Koenigsaecker, George. Leading the Lean Enterprise Transformation. Boca Raton, FL: CRC Press, 2016, 94.

51. Ibid., 94.

52. Storlie, Chad. "Manage Uncertainty with Commander's Intent." https://hbr.org/2010/11/dont-play-golf-in-a-football-g, 2010.

53. "The Effects-Based Approach to Operations." http://www.doctrine.af.mil/Portals/61/documents/Annex_3-0/3-0-D06-OPS-EBAO.pdf, 2016.

54. Sobel, Milo. The 12-Hour MBA. New Jersey: Prentice Hall, 1993, 197.

55. Gerber, Michael E. The E-Myth Revisited. New York: HarperCollins, 1995, 149-150.

56. Belicove, Mikal E. "Understanding Goals, Strategy, Objectives and Tactics in the Age of Social." https://www.forbes.com/sites/mikalbelicove/2013/09/27/understanding-goals-strategies-objectives-and-tactics-in-the-age-of-social/#28d714894c79, 2013

57. Ibid.

58. Harter, Jim. "Obsolete Annual Reviews: Gallup's Advice." http://news.gallup.com/opinion/gallup/185921/obsolete-annual-reviews-gallup-advice.aspx, 2015.

59. Gallo, Amy. "Making Sure Your Employees Succeed." https://hbr.org/2011/02/making-sure-your-employees-suc, 2011.

60. Covey, Stephen R. The 7 Habits of Highly Effective People. New York: Simon & Schuster, 1989, 105.

61. Gerber, Michael. Beyond the E-Myth: The Evolution of an Enterprise. Carlsbad, CA: Michael E. Gerber Companies, 2018, 123 & 125.

62. Gawande, Atul. The Checklist Manifesto. New York: Picador, 2009, 2010, 33-34.

63. Salas, E., Dickinson, T.L., Converse, S.A., and Tannenbaum, S. I., "Toward an understanding of team performance and training. In R.W. Swezey & E. Salas (Eds.) Teams: Their training and performance (pp. 3-29). Norwood, NJ: Ablex, 1992, p. 4 in Salas, Eduardo, Marissa L. Shuffler, Amanda L. Thayer, Wendy L. Bedwell, and Elizabeth H. Lazzara. "Understanding and Improving Teamwork in Organizations: A Scientifically Based Practical Guide". Human Resource Management, Wiley Periodicals, Inc., 2014.

64. Katzenbach, Jon R. and Smith, Douglas K. The Wisdom of Teams. Boston, MA: Harvard Business Review Press, 1993, 16.

65. Salas, Eduardo, Marissa L. Shuffler, Amanda L. Thayer, Wendy L. Bedwell, and Elizabeth H. Lazzara. "Understanding and Improving Teamwork in Organizations: A Scientifically Based Practical Guide". Human Resource Management, Wiley Periodicals, Inc., 2014.

66. Wildman, J.L., Thayer, A.L., Rosen, M.A., Salas, E., Mathieu, J.E. & Rayne, S.R. "Task types and team-level attributes: Synthesis of team classification literature. Human Resource Development Review, 11, 97-129, 2012, in Salas, Eduardo, Marissa L. Shuffler, Amanda L. Thayer, Wendy L. Bedwell, and Elizabeth H. Lazzara. "Understanding and Improving Teamwork in Organizations: A Scientifically Based Practical Guide". Human Resource Management, Wiley Periodicals, Inc., 2014.

67. Morgan, B.B., Salas, E., & Glickman, A.S., An analysis of team evolution and maturation. Journal of General Psychology, 120(3), 277-291, 1994, in Salas, Eduardo, Marissa L. Shuffler, Amanda L. Thayer, Wendy L. Bedwell, and Elizabeth H. Lazzara. "Understanding and Improving Teamwork in Organizations: A Scientifically Based Practical Guide". Human Resource Management, Wiley Periodicals, Inc., 2014.

68. Salas, E.L., Reyes, Denise L., McDaniel, Susan H., "The Science of Teamwork: Progress, Reflections, and the Road Ahead" American Psychologist Vol. 73, No. 4, 2018.

69. Lacey, Joyce W. and Stark, Craig E.L.. "The Neuroscience of Memory: Implications for the Courtroom." https://www.ncbi.nlm.nih.gov/pmc/articles/PMC4183265/, 2013.

70. Ibid.

71. Ibid.

72. Salas, Eduardo, Marissa L. Shuffler, Amanda L. Thayer, Wendy L. Bedwell, and Elizabeth H. Lazzara. "Understanding and Improving Teamwork in Organizations: A Scientifically Based Practical Guide". Human Resource Management, Wiley Periodicals, Inc., 2014.

73. Website: https://www.ahrq.gov/teamstepps/index.html

74. Brenner, Abigail M.D., "The Benefits of Creative Visualization", https://www.psychologytoday.com/us/blog/in-flux/201606/the-benefits-creative-visualization, 2016.

75. Website: https://debriefnow.com/what-is-a-debrief/do-debriefs-work.html.

76. Kerth, Norman. Project Retrospectives. New York, NY: Dorset House Publishing Co., Inc., 2001, 7.

77. Reyes, Tannenbaum, and Salas. "Team Development: The Power of Debriefing." People + Strategy, Spring 2018.

78. Collins, Jim. Good to Great. New York: HarperCollins Publishers Inc., 2001, 20.

79. Duke, Annie. Thinking in Bets. New York: Penguin, 2018, 8.

80. Ibid., 10.

81. Ibid., 35.

82. Reyes, Tannenbaum, and Salas. "Team Development: The Power of Debriefing." People + Strategy, Spring 2018.

83. Website: http://www.criticalthinking.org/pages/our-conception-of-critical-thinking/411.

84. Duke, Annie. Thinking in Bets. New York: Penguin, 2018, 27.

85. Website: https://www.mindtools.com/pages/article/newTMC_5W.htm

86. Koenigsaecker, George. Leading the Lean Enterprise Transformation. Boca Raton, FL: CRC Press, 2016, 116.

87. Ibid., 116.

88. Website: https://www.mindtools.com/pages/article/newTMC_01.htm.

89. Usmani, Fahad. "Fishbone (Cause and Effect or Ishikawa) Diagram." Blog: https://pmstudycircle.com/2014/07/fishbone-cause-and-effect-or-ishikawa-diagram/, 2015.

90. U.S. Department of Defense. The Armed Forces Officer. Virginia: National Defense University Press and Potomac Books, Inc.,2007, 66.

91. Ibid., 66.

92. Ibid., 66-67.

93. Reyes, Tannenbaum, and Salas. "Team Development: The Power of Debriefing." People + Strategy, Spring 2018.

94. Reyes, Tannenbaum, and Salas. "Team Development: The Power of Debriefing." People + Strategy, Spring 2018.

95. Tannenbaum, S.I. & Cerasoli, C.P. (2013). Do team and individual debriefs enhance performance? A meta-analysis. Human Factors: The Journal of Human Factors and Ergonomics Society, 55, 231-245.

96. https://www.groupoe.com/images/Debriefs_-_An_Experiential_Learning_Tool_-_White_Paper.pdf.

97. Ibid.

98. Richards, Chet. Certain to Win. Bloomington, IN: Xlibris Corp., 2004, 136-137.

99. Army Doctrine Reference Publication (ADRP) 3-0, Unified Land Operations (Washington, DC: Government Printing Office [GPO], May 2012), 2 19.

100. Maercellin, Jean Denis. The Pilot Factor. Hamilton, ON, Canada: Plane&Simple Solutions, 2014, 49.

101. Katzenbach, Jon R. and Smith, Douglas K. The Wisdom of Teams. Boston, MA: Harvard Business Review Press, 1993, 16.

THERE'S MUCH MORE TO TEAMWORK THAN BRINGING SMART PEOPLE TOGETHER. THERE'S AN ACTUAL SCIENCE TO WHY SOME TEAMS WIN, AND OTHERS DON'T.

 20-25% Better Teamwork Processes = 20-25% more likely that the team succeeds[1]

 20-25% Teams that practice effective debriefs = 20-25% performance boost[2]

 5% Organizations that boost collaborative performance = 5% greater annual revenue increases[3]

HOW WE SERVE YOU

▸ Top Gun Leadership System Workshops (½-day, Full-day & 2-Day)

▸ Keynotes (Business & Motivation)

▸ Coaching (Custom-tailored)

▸ Consulting

▸ Web-based follow-up | Online Training (coming Fall of 2019)

TESTIMONIALS:

"I really appreciated the training! This is a topic I had little understanding of and now feel much more prepared to implement some of the strategies!"
Mark S., Business Principal

"Excellent instruction and content. There is a lot to take in, but it will pay big dividends!"
Samantha R., Business Principal

"Great content and presentation, genuine leadership, very pragmatic for real world application."
Carlos E., Business Principal

"With follow through, these insights can change companies, as it has changed the Air Force and Armed Forces."
Rebecca M., Business Principal

WE ARE

▸ Top Gun Experts: People who lived what we teach, and became qualified (not certified) to do so.

▸ Business Leaders: Former and current CEOs, marketing and sales professionals, and engineers.

▸ A Team of Teams: Partners through Next-Generation Edge(TM) with AGLX and Cynefin.io.

▸ YOUR Partner in Growth: Helping you and your teams achieve and maintain organizational excellence.

Learn more about Top Gun Leadership in:
TEAM TO SUCCEED

Available at Amazon.com and wherever fine books are sold

SOME OF OUR RECENT CLIENTS:

PATRIOT MISSION • Northwestern Mutual • VISTAGE • DAU

1 LePine, et. Al., 2008 in https://www.gvsu.edu/cms4/asset/CC22E6AB-DC19-6BE8-D720C9DBBEEBBAD3/sales_-_miparc_presentation_final_9-21-17.pdf
2 Tannenbaum & Ceresull, 2013 in https://www.gvsu.edu/cms4/asset/CC22E6AB-DC19-6BE8-D720E90BBEEBBAD3/sales_-_miparc_presentation_final_9-21-17.pdf
3 Corporate Executive Board, 2013 in https://www.gvsu.edu/cms4/asset/CC22E6AB-DC19-6BE8-D720EX0BBEEBBAD3/sales_-_miparc_presentation_final_9-21-17.pdf